100 AMAZING FACTS ABOUT ATHLETICS

2024, Marc Dresgui

Index

" The important thing in life is not the triumph, but the fight; The most important thing is not to have won, but to have fought well."

- Pierre de Coubertin

Introduction

Welcome to the fascinating world of athletics! This book is an invitation to discover 100 Amazing Facts that have marked the history of this sport, from its ancient origins to contemporary records. Through these pages, you'll explore the exploits of the greatest athletes, as well as the lesser-known stories that make this discipline so fascinating.

Athletics, often referred to as "the king of sports", is much more than a simple competition of strength or speed. It's a blend of endurance, technique, strategy and, above all, self-transcendence. Every record broken, every race won bears witness to the extraordinary potential of the human body.

You'll discover the surprising anecdotes behind some of the most impressive records. For example, did you know that the marathon distance we know today is the result of a last-minute adjustment to satisfy a request from the British royal family? These are the kinds of stories we'll be exploring together.

This book will also give you a better understanding of the technological innovations that have transformed athletics, from revolutionary footwear to performance-optimized track surfaces. These developments have enabled athletes to push back the boundaries of what's possible, and you to better understand how.

So get ready to travel through the milestones, legends and mysteries of athletics. Each page will bring you a new perspective on this timeless sport, and, perhaps, a new admiration for those champions who have redefined the history of sport.

Fact 1 - The first marathon of the modern Olympic Games (1896)

At the first modern Olympic Games, held in Athens in 1896, the marathon became a must-do event. The idea for the race was inspired by a Greek legend telling the story of Philippides, an Athenian soldier. According to this legend, he ran from the city of Marathon to Athens, a distance of around 40 km, to announce the Greek victory over the Persians in 490 B.C. This story prompted the Games organizers to recreate a similar endurance race to pay tribute to this legendary feat.

On April 10, 1896, twenty-five Greek and foreign runners lined up at the start of this first Olympic marathon, which covered a slightly shorter distance than today's marathon. The course linked the town of Marathon to the Panathenaic Stadium in Athens. The participants included runners of many different nationalities, but the Greeks were particularly motivated, as they saw the race as a symbol of their historical heritage.

The race was won by a Greek, Spiridon Louis, a 23-year-old water carrier. He became a national hero after crossing the finish line in 2 hours, 58 minutes and 50 seconds. His triumphant arrival in the Panathenaic stadium to the cheers of the crowd was the stuff of legend. It was a moment of immense pride for Greece, to see one of its compatriots win a race inspired by its history.

Organizing the first marathon posed a number of logistical challenges. Runners had to contend with a difficult, hilly course under a scorching sun. The lack of hydration and preparation, by modern standards, made the race particularly demanding for participants. Nevertheless, the event was a resounding success and helped establish the marathon as a legendary sporting event.

Since then, the marathon has become an emblematic event at the Olympic Games and other major athletics competitions around the world. The official marathon distance was later set at 42.195 km, at the 1908 London Games. But it all began on this day in Athens, in 1896, in a race that marked the history of athletics forever.

Fact 2 - The 100m world record: Usain Bolt

On August 16, 2009, Jamaican sprinter Usain Bolt made athletics history by setting a new world record in the 100-meter dash at the World Championships in Berlin. He covered the distance in 9.58 seconds, a time that seems almost unreal given the spectacular nature of his performance. To this day, the record is unsurpassed and has made Bolt a living legend of sprinting, a feat many consider to be one of the sport's greatest moments.

To understand Bolt's incredible speed, imagine running at an average of around 37.58 km/h, with a peak of almost 44.72 km/h! He outclassed his rivals right from the start, and his exceptional stride, with its impressive amplitude, enabled him to open up a significant gap from the very first meters. This performance was made even more incredible by his near-perfect running technique, combining power and release.

Usain Bolt didn't just break a record, he dominated the event with disconcerting ease. He had already made his mark the previous year, in 2008, at the Beijing Olympics, winning the gold medal with a record time of 9.69 seconds. But in Berlin, he pushed his own limits. Shortly before the race, he was already considered the favorite, but nobody expected such an improvement in his own time.

The 100-meter dash is often referred to as the "world's fastest race", as it puts athletes' raw speed and physical capabilities to the test. Bolt not only won the race, he redefined what was thought to be humanly possible. This performance is all the more impressive given that very few athletes have come close to this time, making Bolt a unique athlete in the history of athletics.

The impact of this record goes far beyond the simple stopwatch. It inspired a new generation of athletes and proved that there are still limits to human speed. Usain Bolt's charisma and performance have made him a global icon, and his record of 9.58 seconds remains an absolute benchmark in the world of athletics.

Fact 3 - Athletes who have run a marathon in under 2 hours

Running a marathon in under two hours seemed, for decades, to be an unattainable goal for athletes. However, on October 12, 2019, in Vienna, world-renowned Kenyan runner Eliud Kipchoge became the first man to break this mythical barrier. In a special attempt organized by the INEOS 1:59 project, he ran the 42.195 kilometers in 1 hour, 59 minutes and 40 seconds. This time is not officially recognized as a world record due to the particular conditions of the race, but the feat remains monumental.

What makes Kipchoge's performance so special is the meticulous preparation and optimal conditions put in place to maximize his chances. Hares, runners who took it in turns to accompany him to maintain the pace, were used, as well as a perfectly flat course. Weather conditions were also ideal, with cool temperatures to minimize thermal effort. Everything was orchestrated for Kipchoge to achieve this time, but the athlete still had to be able to pull it off, and that's exactly what he did.

Kipchoge is one of the greatest marathon runners in history. He already held the official world record with a time of 2 hours, 1 minute and 39 seconds, set at the 2018 Berlin Marathon. This record was validated by the official authorities, as the race took place under regular competitive conditions. However, it was his two minutes slower time in Vienna that captured the imagination of the whole world, as it pushed back what were thought to be human limits.

This feat has been compared to other great moments in sporting history, such as the first man to run a mile (1,609 metres) in under 4 minutes, achieved by Roger Bannister in 1954. Running a marathon in under two hours is a feat of endurance, speed and mastery of the human body, just as the sub-4-minute mile was for the previous generation.

It's important to note that Kipchoge's performance is unique and has yet to be reproduced in an official competition. However, it remains etched in the sport's history and has paved the way for a new generation of runners who dream of achieving what many thought impossible: running a marathon in under two hours in a recognized competition.

Fact 4 - The youngest Olympic champion in athletics

In 1896, at the first modern Olympic Games in Athens, a 17-year-old athlete named Dimitrios Loundras won the bronze medal in gymnastics, but the youngest Olympic track and field champion was another prodigy. He is Bob Mathias, an American who, at just 17, became Olympic decathlon champion in 1948. This incredible Fact made history, as the decathlon is considered one of the most demanding disciplines in athletics, combining ten events of endurance, strength and technique.

Bob Mathias' victory at the 1948 London Olympics is all the more impressive given that he began training for the decathlon only a few months before the Games. Mathias, originally from Tulare, California, had to learn and master several events, some of which were completely unknown to him. This shows just how exceptional his athletic potential and adaptability were, especially for a teenager.

During the competition, Mathias not only beat competitors far more experienced than himself, but also had to contend with difficult weather conditions. The two-day decathlon features a variety of events, from the 100-meter dash to the javelin throw, pole vault and 1500-meter run. Despite his young age and lack of experience, Mathias overcame fatigue and pressure to win the gold medal.

What makes Mathias' achievement even more remarkable is that he then returned to the 1952 Olympic Games in Helsinki, where he not only defended his title, but did so with even clearer dominance. He thus became the first athlete to win back-to-back gold medals in the decathlon, cementing his status as an athletics legend.

Bob Mathias' story inspires generations of athletes, and shows that even at a young age, it's possible to achieve extraordinary feats in the world of athletics. His youth and determination have left their mark on the history of the Olympic Games, and his name will forever be associated with sporting excellence.

Fact 5 - The incredible history of hurdling

Hurdling, now one of the most technical disciplines in athletics, has surprising origins. It originated in 19th-century England, where Oxford students began running by jumping over wooden fences, similar to the hurdles used to demarcate fields. The purpose of this race was to make training more difficult and exciting, but nobody imagined at the time that it would become an essential Olympic discipline.

The first hurdles used were rigid and didn't fall when an athlete hit them, making them much more dangerous than those we know today. In 1864, the first official hurdling competition took place in England, with a distance of 120 yards (about 110 meters). The wooden hurdles represented a real challenge, and runners not only had to run fast, but also avoid tripping over these immovable obstacles.

The development of hurdling accelerated with the Olympic Games. The 110-meter hurdles event for men appeared at the first modern Games in 1896. Later, women's events were introduced, notably the 80-meter hurdles in 1932, replaced in 1972 by the 100-meter hurdles. This change made it possible to better align men's and women's competitions, while maintaining the technical challenges specific to this race.

The most amazing thing about hurdling is the incredible technique it requires. Unlike other sprint events, where only speed counts, hurdlers have to adjust their stride perfectly so as not to lose time jumping. Hurdle heights vary from category to category, but the principle remains the same: clear ten hurdles while maintaining a fast, steady running pace.

Among the champions of this discipline, we particularly remember Edwin Moses, the American who dominated the 400-meter hurdles in the 1970s and 1980s. He won 122 consecutive races and broke two world records, making him one of the greatest hurdlers of all time. His fluid style and steady strides enabled him to push the limits of this demanding sport. Today, hurdling remains a spectacular event that demands both power and precision.

Fact 6 - The bizarre rules of ancient javelin throwing

Javelin throwing, an essential discipline in modern athletics, has its origins in ancient Greece. However, the rules of throwing back then were very different from those of today. The ancient Greeks practiced javelin throwing as part of the pentathlon, but it wasn't just about distance. The javelin had to hit specific targets, often placed at different distances, and precision was as important as strength.

One of the most surprising rules concerned the use of a strap called ankyle, attached to the middle of the javelin. Athletes wrapped it around their fingers to give the weapon a spin as they threw it. This rotational effect enabled the javelin to travel longer distances with a more stable trajectory, but it also made the throw more technical and difficult to master. This technique has completely disappeared in modern athletics, where only momentum and arm strength determine the throw.

Another peculiarity of the ancient javelin throw was that athletes were judged not only on the distance covered, but also on their posture and elegance during the throw. It wasn't enough to throw far, it had to be done aesthetically. The Greeks valued harmony of body and movement, and each athlete was judged on his or her ability to throw the javelin gracefully, adding an artistic dimension to the competition.

In some competitions, athletes were even required to throw the javelin while running on a horse! This rule, which seems totally absurd today, combined the mastery of throwing with that of horsemanship. Rider-athletes had to control their mount while throwing with precision, a feat requiring strength, coordination and an excellent sense of balance. It was a true demonstration of versatility and multiple skills.

These strange and forgotten rules show that javelin throwing wasn't always about brute strength. It was a complex sport, requiring a combination of skill, technique and even elegance. Although these rules have evolved to focus more on distance and accuracy, they remind us how early athletics competitions were influenced by values very different from those of today.

Fact 7 - How Jesse Owens made history in 1936

In 1936, at the Olympic Games in Berlin, Jesse Owens wrote one of the most memorable pages in the history of athletics. This American athlete won four gold medals, a feat that remains engraved in the annals of sport. Owens triumphed in sprint and long jump events, breaking impressive records each time. What makes his feat even more incredible is the context in which he achieved it: these Olympic Games were being held in Germany under the Nazi regime, a regime that promoted racist theories of superiority.

Jesse Owens won gold in the 100-meter dash, the event that crowns the world's fastest man, with an exceptional time of 10.3 seconds. It was a stunning victory, but only the first in a series. Two days later, he also triumphed in the long jump with a leap of 8.06 metres, setting a new Olympic record. This feat was all the more remarkable in that it came after Owens had almost failed to qualify at the trials.

Owens didn't just shine in the individual events. He also contributed to the American team's victory in the 4x100-meter relay, where his team set a new world record in 39.8 seconds. His fourth medal came in the 200 meters, which he won by a comfortable margin, consolidating his dominance in the sprint events. Every Jesse Owens performance was marked by technical ease and lightning speed.

His success resonated around the world, not only for the quality of his performances, but also for their symbolic significance. Owens, an African-American athlete, not only proved that he was one of the finest sportsmen of his time, but also highlighted the absurdity of the racial theories advocated by the Nazi regime. The spectators at Berlin's Olympic Stadium, including the dignitaries in attendance, had no choice but to admire the excellence of this athlete.

Jesse Owens' legacy goes far beyond his four gold medals. His example has inspired generations of athletes around the world, showing that determination and talent can transcend all barriers, be they political or social. He has become a symbol of courage, excellence and equality, leaving an indelible mark on the history of the Olympic Games and athletics.

Fact 8 - The marathon runner who ran barefoot

At the 1960 Olympic Games in Rome, a surprising event went down in marathon history. Abebe Bikila, an Ethiopian athlete, became the first African to win a marathon gold medal, and he did so barefoot. This unusual choice was not a decision planned in advance. The day before the race, Bikila tried on several pairs of shoes, but none suited him. Rather than risk injury with ill-fitting shoes, he chose to run as he often trained: shoeless.

The course of the Rome Marathon was not an easy one, but Bikila, with his light stride and exceptional endurance, impressed the world. As he covered the 42.195 kilometers through the Eternal City, he maintained a steady pace, outclassing his rivals. In the final kilometers, he accelerated away from Morocco's Rhadi Ben Abdesselam, crossing the finish line in 2 hours, 15 minutes and 16 seconds, a new Olympic record at the time.

The choice to run barefoot wasn't just a question of comfort. Bikila had grown up in the mountains of Ethiopia, where he was used to running without shoes. This had enabled him to develop a natural running technique and impressive stamina. His choice to remain faithful to this method, even at an event as prestigious as the Olympic Games, reinforced his image as an exceptional runner, mastering both body and mind.

Bikila's triumphant finish under the Arch of Constantine, one of Rome's most emblematic monuments, was an unforgettable moment. Not only did he break a record, he also showed the world that it was possible to win such a difficult race without the equipment usually considered indispensable. Abebe Bikila has become an athletics legend and a source of inspiration for generations of athletes.

Four years later, Bikila repeated his feat at the Tokyo Olympics, this time wearing shoes. He became the first athlete to win back-to-back marathon gold medals, proving that his talent went far beyond his incredible barefoot victory in Rome. His story remains one of the most fascinating in Olympic history, symbolizing tenacity and excellence in the most unexpected moments.

Fact 9 - The longest cross-country run ever made

There's a lot more to athletics than fast races and sprint events. Among long-distance races, one of the most incredible is the 1928 transcontinental race, often referred to as "The Bunion Derby". This extraordinary race, held in the United States, consisted of running 5,523 kilometers from Los Angeles to New York. Over 200 runners set off, and only 55 crossed the finish line after 84 days of intense effort.

The idea for this race was born in the mind of C.C. Pyle, a promoter in search of new spectacles. It was an unprecedented endurance race, where participants had to run almost 80 kilometers a day, under extreme weather conditions, crossing deserts, mountains and plains. The event was particularly challenging, as the riders had only rudimentary equipment compared with modern standards.

The winner of this monumental race was a Native American named Andy Payne. Originally from Oklahoma, Payne had decided to enter the race to help his family pay off the mortgage on their farm. Despite physical pain and exhaustion, he persisted day after day, beating all other competitors and winning the sum of $25,000, a small fortune at the time.

This race not only tested the physical limits of the runners, but also their mental endurance. Many gave up along the way, unable to cope with the injuries, fatigue and climate. Those who managed to complete this legendary race proved that they possessed extraordinary tenacity, making it one of the longest and toughest races in the history of athletics.

The transcontinental race of 1928 remains an unrivalled achievement in the history of long-distance running. It marked the history of athletics for its duration, distance and the incredible prowess of those who completed it. This event shows just how far human endurance can be tested in extreme conditions, and illustrates the courage of the athletes who set out on this epic adventure.

Fact 10 - The incredible Jamaican 4x100m relay runners

The Jamaican 4x100-meter relay has become a legend in world athletics, thanks in no small part to breathtaking performances at the Olympic Games and World Championships. Jamaica's men's team, with stars such as Usain Bolt, Asafa Powell and Yohan Blake, dominated this event for many years, breaking incredible records. One of the most memorable moments remains the London 2012 Olympic Games final, where Jamaica not only won gold, but also set a phenomenal world record of 36.84 seconds.

What makes this performance so spectacular is the fluidity and precision with which the baton is passed from one runner to the next. In such a fast race, a single error in timing can cost victory. Yet the Jamaican team demonstrated a perfect mastery of these exchanges, which largely contributed to their success. Asafa Powell's explosive start, followed by powerful relays from Yohan Blake and Nesta Carter, always set the stage for Usain Bolt's masterful conclusion, which finished the race with a bang.

The Jamaican relay has also made history for its ability to push human limits in terms of sheer speed. At the 2009 World Championships in Berlin, the team had already broken the world record, but it was in London, in 2012, that they reached their peak. Each member of the team was one of the best sprinters of his generation, and together they formed an almost unbeatable team.

The 4x100-meter relay is an event that demands both speed and coordination. Unlike individual races, it's teamwork that makes the difference here. The Jamaicans succeeded in raising this cooperation to a level of excellence rarely achieved. Their performances not only captivated audiences around the world, but also marked an era when Jamaica dominated world sprinting.

This reign over the 4x100 metres confirmed Jamaica as one of the greatest breeding grounds for sprinters in the history of athletics. The Jamaican men's team, thanks to its impressive cohesion and exceptional individual talents, remains to this day a benchmark for future generations, and their records continue to inspire athletes the world over.

Fact 11 - Fosbury's high jump record

In 1968, at the Olympic Games in Mexico City, Dick Fosbury, a young American athlete, revolutionized high jumping by introducing a totally new technique. While most jumpers were still using the "scissors" or "belly roll" style, Fosbury surprised everyone with his "Fosbury flop". He cleared the bar with his back first, a method that would change the discipline forever. The jump won him the gold medal with a height of 2.24 meters, an Olympic record at the time.

Fosbury's technique consisted of running in a curve, then jumping so as to pass the bar from behind, head first, legs last. This counter-intuitive but effective method enabled him to make better use of gravitational force and distribute his weight in such a way as to clear heights impossible with traditional techniques. Although this approach was initially mocked and considered unorthodox, it soon became the dominant method in high jumping.

Fosbury began developing this technique in high school, as he was unable to succeed with conventional methods. It was only by dint of experimentation that he perfected the "flop" and succeeded in using it competitively. At the Mexico Olympic Games, where the track and vault were designed with softer surfaces than before, his technique proved particularly advantageous, offering him a greater margin of safety in the event of a fall.

The "Fosbury flop" not only helped Dick Fosbury become Olympic champion, it also transformed the way high jumping is practiced. Today, almost all high jump athletes use this technique. The radical change it brought to the sport is comparable to a veritable technical revolution, enabling athletes to clear ever more impressive heights.

Fosbury's impact on athletics goes far beyond his Olympic title. By introducing this new approach, he redefined what was thought possible in the discipline. His record of 2.24 metres was just the beginning of the Fosbury flop's domination of the world stage, proving that innovation can change the course of sporting history forever.

Fact 12 - The evolution of the pole vault

Pole vaulting is an impressive discipline that combines strength, agility and technique. However, one of the keys to success in this event is the pole itself, which has evolved considerably over the decades. Initially, the poles used were made of wood, often ash or bamboo, rigid materials that didn't allow much flexibility. This limited the height athletes could reach, as wooden poles broke easily under pressure.

In the 1940s, metal poles made their appearance, offering greater durability. However, they remained relatively heavy and rigid, which still didn't allow athletes to exploit their full power. These early metal poles, often made of aluminum, allowed some progress, but were not flexible enough to fundamentally change the discipline.

The big revolution came in the 1960s with the introduction of fiberglass poles. This material, both lightweight and highly flexible, transformed the way athletes approached the discipline. For the first time, poles bent under the pressure exerted by the jumper, allowing them to store energy and then release it to propel the athlete even higher. This led to a veritable explosion in world records, as fiberglass poles opened up new possibilities in terms of technique and height reached.

As technology has evolved, poles have continued to improve. Today, they are mainly made of carbon fiber, an even lighter and stronger material. These poles enable athletes to achieve spectacular performances by combining extreme flexibility with impressive durability. Thanks to these innovations, high jumpers can now reach heights previously unimaginable.

The evolution of the pole has been a determining factor in the history of pole vaulting. From wooden poles to today's carbon-fiber models, each technological advance has enabled athletes to push back the limits of the sport. Legends such as Sergei Bubka, who broke the world record several times in the 1980s and 1990s, took advantage of these advances to raise the level of the discipline and turn it into a veritable spectacle of technique and power.

Fact 13 - Track and field competitions under stormy skies

Athletics competitions are often synonymous with blue skies and ideal conditions, but sometimes athletes have to contend with far more unpredictable elements, such as violent storms. One of the most memorable of these took place during the 1964 Tokyo Olympics, when the track and field finals were marred by torrential rain. Soggy tracks, combined with strong winds, made every run and jump even more difficult, forcing athletes to adapt their technique.

Despite these extreme conditions, the performances were no less spectacular. In the 100-meter event, for example, the sprinters had to run in driving rain that made the track slippery. Nevertheless, some incredible records were set. American Bob Hayes won the gold medal with a time of 10.06 seconds, breaking an Olympic record. This performance was made all the more impressive by the fact that he ran in a straight line, with the track flooded, and finished several meters ahead of his rivals.

The jumping events were not spared by the storm. In the long jump, athletes had to adjust their momentum to cope with the wet track and strong wind. Britain's Lynn Davies, nicknamed "Bouncing Lynn", won the gold medal with a jump of 8.07 meters, a feat in such difficult conditions. This jump has become a symbol of the resilience of athletes in the face of natural elements.

Similar storms have also marked other athletics events. In 1993, during the World Athletics Championships in Stuttgart, a severe storm interrupted several events, forcing the organizers to change the schedule. The finals were held under dark skies and incessant rain. However, this did not prevent the athletes from delivering top-level performances, illustrating the human capacity to overcome unforeseen obstacles.

Track and field competitions in stormy weather show just how much more this sport requires than speed and strength. Adapting to the natural elements, whether rain, wind or even extreme temperatures, puts athletes' physical and mental stamina to the test. And it's often in these moments that the most legendary performances are born, as they testify to an athlete's ability to excel whatever the conditions.

Fact 14 - The fastest race ever recorded

On August 16, 2009, at the World Athletics Championships in Berlin, Usain Bolt achieved a performance that will go down in history. By running the 100 meters in just 9.58 seconds, he broke his own world record and established what is now the fastest race ever recorded. This performance stunned the world, not only for the speed achieved, but also for the apparent ease with which Bolt achieved it.

Incredibly, Bolt ran at an average speed of 37.58 km/h, peaking at 44.72 km/h during the race. These figures are almost unimaginable when you think of normal human speed. For the spectators in Berlin's Olympic Stadium, it was a breathtaking spectacle. Bolt won by a considerable margin over his rivals, finishing several meters ahead of them.

Part of this success is due to Bolt's unique technique. His size, unusual for a sprinter (he's 1.95 metres tall), gives him an exceptional stride. Whereas other sprinters have to take many more strides to cover the distance, Bolt takes fewer, but with impressive amplitude. This combination of power, speed and elegance has made him an outstanding athlete, capable of pushing back the limits of human speed.

This was not Bolt's first exploit. The previous year, at the 2008 Beijing Olympics, he had already broken the world record for the 100 metres in 9.69 seconds. But in Berlin, he surpassed his own performance and that of all the other athletes, making a permanent mark on the history of the sport. On that day, athletics set a new standard for speed.

Usain Bolt's feat not only rewrote the record books, it also inspired generations of athletes to aim for the impossible. Since then, no runner has yet managed to break the record, and many wonder how long it will be before someone manages to break the 9.58-second barrier. But be that as it may, Bolt's run in Berlin remains the fastest ever recorded, a moment of pure magic in the history of athletics.

Fact 15 - The revolutionary running shoes of the 2000s

The 2000s marked a turning point in athletics, thanks in large part to the arrival of revolutionary running shoes. While athletic performance had always been the result of rigorous training and exceptional physical ability, new technologies applied to footwear offered runners an added advantage. These shoes, developed by brands such as Nike and Adidas, featured special soles designed to maximize energy restitution and improve athletes' speed.

One of the most famous models, the Nike Vaporfly, introduced in 2017, was a game-changer for marathon runners. Featuring a carbon fiber plate integrated into the sole, they enabled more efficient propulsion during the stride, while reducing muscle fatigue. This innovative design helped many athletes beat their personal records. In fact, at the 2018 Berlin Marathon, Eliud Kipchoge, who wore these shoes, set a new world record with a time of 2 hours, 1 minute and 39 seconds.

These new shoes not only improved speed, they were also designed to offer runners greater comfort and stability. The sole material, often an ultra-light foam, better absorbed shock and reduced the risk of injury. The performance achieved with these shoes was quickly debated, with some believing they offered an "unfair technological advantage". In spite of this, they were approved by international bodies and became an essential choice for top-level marathoners and sprinters.

Another major development in the shoes of the 2000s was the attention paid to lightness. Manufacturers sought to design running shoes that were as light as possible, while retaining good cushioning and excellent grip. For example, the extremely lightweight Adidas Adizero was used in sprint and marathon competitions, offering a perfect compromise between comfort and performance.

The impact of these revolutionary running shoes on athletics cannot be underestimated. By enabling athletes to exploit their physical potential to the full, they have contributed to a proliferation of records in top-level competitions. These innovations, combined with the natural talent of our runners, have redefined what is possible in the world of athletics.

Fact 16 - The first women's Olympic record in athletics

In 1928, at the Amsterdam Olympic Games, the history of women's athletics was marked by a decisive breakthrough: women were finally able to take part in several athletics events, something that had not been allowed before. Among these first competitions, the women's 100 metres became one of the most closely followed. It was on this occasion that Betty Robinson, a 16-year-old American athlete, made history by winning the first women's gold medal in this event, setting the first-ever women's Olympic record.

Betty Robinson ran the distance in 12.2 seconds, an exceptional time for the time. Her victory not only marked a turning point for women in the sport, but also revealed to the world the potential of female athletes in sprint competitions. Robinson, who had only begun training seriously a few months before the Games, quickly became an emblematic figure of this first female participation in Olympic track and field events.

Robinson's 100m was not the only event in which women shone at these Games, but her feat had a special resonance. It proved that women were just as capable as men of pushing their physical limits in the most demanding disciplines. At the time, opportunities for women to compete in athletics were rare, and Robinson's performance played a crucial role in changing the perception of female athletes around the world.

Betty Robinson was not only fast, she was also persevering. After her 1928 feat, she continued to run, but her career was brought to an abrupt halt by a plane crash in 1931, in which she was seriously injured. It took her several years to recover, but she made an incredible comeback by winning another gold medal in the 4x100-meter relay at the 1936 Berlin Olympics, proving once again her determination and talent.

The story of the first women's Olympic record, set by Betty Robinson, paved the way for generations of female athletes to follow. Her feat is remembered as a key moment in the emancipation of women in sport, and continues to inspire those who dream of breaking barriers and reaching the top in the world of athletics.

Fact 17 - Hammer throwing techniques through the ages

Hammer throwing, one of the most impressive disciplines in athletics, has evolved considerably over the centuries, both in technique and in the equipment used. Originally, this event has its roots in Celtic traditions, where men threw real iron hammers to demonstrate their strength. Over time, the event evolved into a discipline of athletics, but the techniques and implements were refined to optimize throwing distance.

In the first modern competitions, at the beginning of the 20th century, the technique consisted mainly of a stationary throw. The athlete would spin once or twice before releasing the hammer. In those days, the hammer was attached to a rigid shaft and rotations were limited. Athletes relied mainly on their brute strength to send the hammer as far as possible. However, this technique had its limits, as without good control of the movement, it was difficult to generate enough speed to achieve exceptional throws.

It was in the 1920s that hammer throwing technique underwent a revolution with the introduction of multiple rotations. Instead of limiting themselves to one or two rotations, athletes began to perform three or four rapid rotations to increase the hammer's speed before releasing it. This technique enabled throwers to make better use of their momentum and maximize distance. The metal pole and flexible cable linking the ball to the handle also improved the precision and power of the throws.

In the 1950s and 1960s, athletes like American Hal Connolly refined these rotation techniques to achieve record distances. Connolly used a technique known as "low stance", which involved keeping his center of gravity as low as possible during rotations, enabling him to better control the trajectory of the hammer while maximizing the force generated. His innovations pushed back the records of the time, and he won the gold medal at the 1956 Olympic Games with an impressive throw of 63.19 meters.

Today, hammer throwing technique is more complex and refined than ever. Modern athletes combine impressive strength with exceptional coordination and precision. The rotations, often three or four in number, are perfectly synchronized to create a balance between speed and control. Current records exceed 80 meters, a testament to the technical advances in this discipline. The evolution of the hammer throw is a perfect example of human ingenuity in the quest for better sporting performance.

Fact 18 - High altitude athletics races

Running at high altitude, where air is scarcer and oxygen less abundant, is a particular challenge for athletes. This phenomenon directly affects the body's ability to deliver oxygen to the muscles, making performance more difficult. However, high altitude can also offer an unexpected advantage in certain athletics events, particularly sprints and jumps, where air resistance is lower, enabling athletes to reach higher speeds.

One of the most emblematic examples of high-altitude competition is undoubtedly the 1968 Olympic Games in Mexico City. Held at 2,240 meters above sea level, these Games saw a series of spectacular records. Bob Beamon, in one of the long jump's most legendary performances, shattered the world record with a leap of 8.90 meters, a record that remained unbroken for almost 23 years. Beamon attributed his extraordinary leap in part to altitude conditions.

For sprinters, the low air density at high altitude reduces resistance, enabling faster performances. At the same Games, incredible records were broken in the sprint events, notably by American Jim Hines, who became the first man to run the 100-meter dash in under 10 seconds, with a time of 9.95 seconds. The combination of altitude and technique of these athletes helped create optimal conditions for breaking records.

However, for long-distance races, such as the marathon or 10,000-meter run, conditions at high altitude are much more difficult. The lack of oxygen can cause fatigue more quickly, forcing runners to adapt their strategy to avoid burning out too early. African athletes, particularly those from countries like Ethiopia and Kenya, who regularly train at high altitude, often have an advantage in these competitions due to their natural adaptation to these conditions.

High-altitude racing continues to be used by athletes to improve their endurance. Many train in mountainous regions to prepare their bodies to better handle sea-level events, a phenomenon known as "hypoxia training". This unique aspect of preparation shows that high altitude, while demanding, offers fascinating strategic opportunities for athletes looking to push their limits in competition.

Fact 19 - Athletes who became champions after switching disciplines

Changing disciplines in athletics and becoming champion is a rare feat, but some athletes have succeeded in this incredible challenge. One of the most fascinating stories is that of Daley Thompson, British decathlon legend. Before devoting himself to this ten-discipline combined event, Thompson was a 100-meter specialist. His transition to the decathlon, an event requiring exceptional versatility, enabled him to win two Olympic gold medals in 1980 and 1984, proving that he had mastered much more than just speed.

Another outstanding example is Michael Jordan. Before shining as an athlete in baseball, it was in basketball that Jordan had distinguished himself, although the attempt to make the transition to a totally different discipline was not as successful as for some track and field athletes.

Jackie Joyner-Kersee is another emblematic case of a successful change of discipline. A long jump specialist, she decided to devote herself to the heptathlon, a demanding event that combines seven different disciplines, including the high jump, javelin throw and 800 meters. Joyner-Kersee dominated the heptathlon for over a decade, winning two Olympic gold medals and setting a world record that still stands today. His ability to excel in such a wide range of events shows the extent of his talent and his adaptability.

Ashton Eaton, another decathlete, distinguished himself by dominating the sprint races as well as the throwing and jumping events, a gigantic challenge. He started out as a hurdler before becoming one of the greatest decathletes of all time, winning two Olympic titles and breaking several world records.

Changing disciplines in athletics requires more than just physical skills. It requires mental adaptation, rapid technical learning and the ability to develop new strengths. These champions, through their successful transition, have shown that mastery of athletics is not limited to a single specialty, but can be extended to multiple disciplines with enough determination and hard work.

Fact 20 - Why the marathon distance is 42.195 km

The marathon distance, now set at 42.195 kilometers, wasn't always so precise. When the event was introduced at the first modern Olympic Games in Athens in 1896, it measured around 40 kilometers, a distance meant to commemorate the legend of Philippides, a Greek soldier who is said to have run from the city of Marathon to Athens to announce the victory of the Greeks over the Persians in 490 B.C. This first Olympic race established the tradition, but the exact distance was not yet standardized.

It was in 1908, during the London Olympic Games, that the current distance of 42.195 km was unexpectedly defined. The course was originally planned to be 26 miles (41.843 kilometers), starting at Windsor Castle and finishing at the Olympic Stadium in White City. However, at the request of the British royal family, the start was slightly modified so that the royal children could watch the race from the castle gardens. This added around 385 meters to the course.

The finish line, meanwhile, was placed in front of the royal box in the Olympic stadium, lengthening the distance by a further fifty yards. This anecdotal change took the total distance to 26 miles and 385 yards, or 42.195 kilometers. Although it was not a scientific or sporting decision, this length was retained, as it corresponded precisely to this particular Olympic edition.

It wasn't until 1921 that the International Association of Athletics Federations (IAAF) decided to officially adopt this distance for all marathons. It was chosen as the standard because of the popularity of the London Games and the unique history surrounding the race. Since then, all official marathon competitions worldwide have followed this distance.

Thus, the current marathon distance of 42.195 km is the result of serendipity and a request from the royal family. It's a fascinating anecdote that reminds us that certain sporting traditions are sometimes born of unexpected events, but then become standards that athletes continue to respect and honor at every competition.

Fact 21 - Oldest record still unbroken since the 80s

The oldest athletics world record still unbeaten since the 1980s is that set by Jarmila Kratochvílová over 800 meters. On July 26, 1983, at a competition in Munich, the Czechoslovakian athlete ran the distance in an impressive time of 1 minute 53.28 seconds. This record remains unsurpassed to this day, making Kratochvílová the holder of the oldest world record in a running event.

What makes this record particularly impressive is the significant gap with the performances of contemporary athletes. Very few runners have come close to this time, which makes it all the more mysterious. Kratochvílová, then aged 32, already had an impressive career, but her 800-meter performance that day took the world by surprise. She ran at an average speed of over 23 km/h, maintaining an intense rhythm from start to finish.

Kratochvílová wasn't just an 800-meter specialist. She also excelled in 400-meter races, and her personal best in this distance, set a few days after her 800-meter record, was just as impressive. Yet it was in the 800 metres that her name went down in history. His impeccable technique, combined with extraordinary stamina and physical strength, enabled him to shatter the times at a time when athletic performance was evolving rapidly.

This record has often been the subject of debate, due to Kratochvílová's incredible progress at an age when most athletes experience a decline in performance. Some have questioned the training conditions at the time and the methods used to maximize performance, but the record remains valid today, and no concrete evidence has officially called it into question.

The fact that this record still stands, despite technological and scientific advances in training, proves just how exceptional Jarmila Kratochvílová's performance was in 1983. This record has become a challenge for future generations, a pinnacle of athleticism that many dream of reaching, but which remains out of reach for the time being.

Fact 22 - Sprinters who break records as they age

In athletics, most athletes reach their peak performance in their twenties, but some sprinters defy this rule by breaking records well into their thirties. A notable example is Kim Collins, an athlete from St. Kitts and Nevis, who broke several sprint records in his forties. At the age of 40, he ran the 100 meters in 9.93 seconds, becoming the first man his age to break the 10-second barrier, a stunning performance that stunned the world.

Kim Collins was no newcomer to the scene. He had already won world titles in his youth, but what captivated spectators was his ability to remain competitive well beyond what most considered the end of a sprinter's career. His secret lay in meticulous physical preparation and perfect technical mastery, which enabled him to maintain impressive speed even at an age when most sprinters retire from competition.

Another inspiring example is Jamaican sprint legend Merlene Ottey. She continued to compete at a very high level until the age of 50, taking part in her seventh Olympic Games in Sydney in 2000. Ottey, famous for her longevity and consistency, showed that speed and endurance are not just a matter of age. She remained competitive, winning international medals well into her forties, proving that experience and determination can sometimes rival youth.

These examples show that the science of training and rigorous fitness management enable some sprinters to push back the limits of time. They know how to adapt their running style and preparation to compensate for age-related physical changes, while making use of their extensive competition experience. Collins, for example, explained that his mental approach had evolved greatly with age, enabling him to remain calm and focused, even in moments of high pressure.

These athletes prove that age need not be a barrier to top-level athletic performance. They inspire generations of runners and show that, although youth is often synonymous with speed, it is possible to continue to shine and break records well into your thirties and even forties, as long as you combine passion, discipline and determination.

Fact 23 - The runner who finished a marathon in a wheelchair

In 1975, Bob Hall made history by becoming the first person to complete a marathon in a wheelchair. At a time when competitions for athletes with disabilities were rare, Hall defied the norm by taking part in the prestigious Boston Marathon. He not only finished the race, but also convinced organizers to allow wheelchair athletes to compete officially in the future. His time of 2 hours 58 minutes proved that wheelchair performance is possible in such a demanding race.

Bob Hall's performance was not just a physical feat, but an act of determination and courage. Before his participation, marathons were reserved for able-bodied runners, and no one imagined that a wheelchair could cover the 42.195 kilometers of a marathon. Hall, with his unshakeable will, used a specially designed wheelchair, lighter and more maneuverable than the traditional models of the time. His arrival at the finish line changed perspectives and ushered in a new era for disabled athletes.

After his achievement, marathons, and Boston in particular, incorporated a specific category for wheelchair athletes. This enabled many other athletes, such as Jean Driscoll and Tatyana McFadden, to follow in Hall's footsteps and dominate the marathon scene. What began as an individual effort to push one's own limits soon became an inclusive movement, encouraging the participation of disabled people in endurance competitions.

Bob Hall's story is also a lesson in perseverance. His first attempts at running marathons were met with skepticism, even rejection. However, convinced that his wheelchair could overcome the same obstacles as runners' legs, Hall persevered, proving to all that human abilities go far beyond physical appearances. Today, his feat is celebrated as a pivotal moment in the history of the marathon and Paralympic sport.

Thanks to pioneers like Bob Hall, wheelchair athletes are now regular competitors in marathons the world over. His courage and vision have paved the way for greater recognition and respect for disabled athletes, demonstrating that the true essence of sport lies in determination, whatever the means used to cross the finish line.

Fact 24 - The breathing secrets of long-distance runners

Breathing plays a crucial role in the performance of long-distance runners. Unlike sprinters, who focus on short, explosive efforts, long-distance runners need to maintain a steady pace for long periods. Breathing control therefore becomes a key skill for optimizing endurance and minimizing fatigue. Breathing deeply and in a controlled manner maximizes oxygen intake, essential for fueling the muscles during prolonged effort.

A technique widely used by long-distance runners is diaphragmatic breathing, which allows the lungs to expand and oxygen to flow more freely. This method involves breathing not through the chest, but through the belly. As you inhale deeply, the diaphragm descends, allowing the lungs to fill with air to the maximum. This technique helps avoid shallow, inefficient breathing, which can limit endurance and cause side stitches.

Long-distance runners also need to adapt their breathing to the rhythm of their strides. A common breathing pattern is the "2:2" technique, in which you inhale for two strides and exhale for the next two. This rhythm maintains a constant supply of oxygen and reduces stress on the body. For intense efforts or uphill runs, some athletes adopt a "2:1" pattern, where the exhalation is more frequent, enabling carbon dioxide to be better evacuated.

It's also important for long-distance runners to adapt to environmental conditions. At altitude, where air is scarcer, runners often have to adjust their breathing to compensate for the reduced oxygen supply. Elite athletes, such as those training in Ethiopia or Kenya, develop exceptional lung capacity thanks to their high-altitude training. Their breathing becomes more efficient, enabling them to perform at a high level even on the plains.

Breathing control isn't just about supplying oxygen. It's also a tool for calming the mind and managing stress during a race. Experienced long-distance runners often use their breathing to stay focused and avoid panic at difficult moments. By controlling their breathing, they can maintain a steady pace and stave off fatigue, enabling them to maintain a sustained effort over distances of several dozen kilometers.

Fact 25 - Long jumpers who defy gravity

The long jump is one of athletics' most spectacular disciplines, where athletes seem to defy the laws of gravity. Among the legendary performances, Bob Beamon's at the 1968 Olympic Games in Mexico City is undoubtedly the most memorable. With an incredible leap of 8.90 meters, Beamon shattered the world record of the time by almost 55 centimeters, a feat that left the whole world speechless. This record was dubbed "the jump of the century" and remained unbeaten for 23 years.

What makes Beamon's jump so extraordinary is the combination of several factors, not least Mexico City's high-altitude conditions, but also the strength and speed he generated in his momentum. By launching himself with perfect acceleration and synchronizing every movement of his body, he managed to stay aloft for almost 2 seconds, giving the impression that he was truly defying gravity. The judges even had to adjust their measuring instruments to calculate the exact distance, as it exceeded the expected limits.

Another long jumper to make history is Carl Lewis. During the 1980s and 1990s, Lewis dominated this discipline, winning four consecutive Olympic gold medals from 1984 to 1996. His fluid, powerful style, combined with impressive top speed on the runway, enabled him to reach distances close to Beamon's record. Although Lewis never exceeded Beamon's 8.90 meters, he maintained incredible consistency, winning title after title with unique elegance.

In 1991, Mike Powell achieved the feat of finally beating Beamon's record at the World Championships in Tokyo. With a phenomenal leap of 8.95 meters, Powell took the title of greatest long jump ever recorded. This historic moment took place during one of track and field's greatest battles, when Carl Lewis also jumped a personal best of 8.91 metres, but it wasn't enough to beat Powell that day.

Long jumpers use not only their physical strength, but also a complex technical mastery to optimize every stage of the jump: from the run-up to the landing and the flight phase. Each jump is a precise calculation of speed, height and take-off angle. For these athletes, every jump is a dance with gravity, where the aim is to stay aloft as long as possible while maintaining perfect balance.

Fact 26 - How athletes train in extreme conditions

Elite athletes sometimes train in extreme conditions to improve their performance, whether it's the sweltering heat of the desert, freezing cold or even high altitude. These challenging environments force the body to adapt, enabling athletes to build endurance and resilience. Marathon runners, for example, often choose to train in desert or mountainous regions to simulate the extreme conditions they might encounter during major competitions.

At altitude, the air contains less oxygen, forcing the body to produce more red blood cells to compensate for the lack of available oxygen. Athletes training in areas such as Iten in Kenya or Flagstaff in the USA, at altitudes of over 2,000 metres, develop better lung capacity. Once back down to sea level, this enables them to maintain a high level of endurance, as their bodies are better equipped to use oxygen efficiently.

On the other hand, training in extreme heat, as in Dubai or the deserts of Arizona, tests resistance to dehydration and exhaustion. Runners must learn to manage their internal resources, in particular by controlling their hydration and adjusting their pace to avoid heat stroke. Special clothing, such as cooling suits or breathable fabrics, help protect athletes while allowing them to get used to the tough conditions.

Some athletes, such as endurance specialists, train in cold or damp environments to prepare for competitions in winter or unstable weather conditions. They learn to cope with the effects of intense cold, which can limit muscle flexibility and increase the risk of injury. Breathing control and body heat management become essential to maintain a high level of performance, even in sub-zero temperatures.

Training in extreme conditions pushes athletes to push back the limits of their body and mind. By confronting hostile environments, they acquire exceptional mental and physical strength, enabling them to perform better under normal circumstances. These extra challenges prepare them for the unpredictable, whether they're competing in scorching heat or racing at high altitude.

Fact 27 - The oldest marathoner to finish the race

Fauja Singh, a man of Indian origin, became the world's oldest marathon runner when he completed the Toronto Marathon in 2011 at the incredible age of 100. This feat is unique in the history of athletics and proved that age is no insurmountable obstacle when it comes to pushing human limits. Fauja Singh, nicknamed "The Turbaned Man", covered the 42.195 km in 8 hours, 11 minutes and 6 seconds, finishing the race with unfailing determination.

Fauja Singh's story is all the more inspiring because he didn't start running until much later in life. After losing his wife and son, he turned to running at the age of 89 to overcome his grief. What began as a simple activity to keep fit turned into a passion, and Singh ran several marathons around the world, breaking numerous records in his age category.

At the 2011 Toronto Marathon, Fauja Singh captivated international attention. Despite his advanced age, he crossed the finish line to the cheers of the crowd. He has become an icon not only for athletes, but for all those who see him as a symbol of perseverance and longevity. Singh has often attributed his longevity and endurance to a simple lifestyle, a vegetarian diet and a positive attitude.

Beyond his sporting achievements, Singh is also a model of humility. After his historic marathon, he declared that he had never run for glory or recognition, but simply to stay healthy and inspire others to stay active, whatever their age. Fauja Singh continued to compete in shorter-distance races after officially retiring from marathons at the age of 101, but he remained an iconic figure in athletics.

Fauja Singh's story shows that determination and passion can push back the limits of what was once thought possible. His name will go down in the annals of athletics as the man who proved that there is no age limit for extraordinary feats.

Fact 28 - The 1964 Tokyo Olympics marathon

The 1964 Tokyo Olympic marathon is remembered for many reasons. This edition saw the spectacular victory of Ethiopia's Abebe Bikila, who won his second consecutive Olympic gold medal, becoming the first marathon runner to achieve this feat. Bikila had already made his mark in Rome in 1960 by running barefoot, but this time he wore shoes and set a new Olympic record of 2 hours, 12 minutes and 11 seconds.

What makes this victory even more impressive is that less than six weeks before the race, Bikila had undergone appendicitis surgery. Few thought he would be able to race, let alone defend his title. Yet during the race, he dominated from start to finish, gradually pulling away from his rivals with a calm, steady pace. At the finish, he looked barely tired, even stretching after crossing the finish line, a gesture that stunned the crowd.

The Tokyo Marathon course was demanding, passing through both urban and hilly areas of the Japanese capital. Heat and humidity were also factors, but Bikila managed these conditions perfectly. His strategy was to maintain a steady pace while keeping an eye on his rivals. At the halfway point, he accelerated and quickly distanced his rivals, running the last few kilometers alone in the lead.

Bikila's victory made history not only for its technical and physical aspects, but also because it reinforced Ethiopia's status as a major marathon nation. By winning a gold medal at two consecutive Olympic Games, Bikila paved the way for other great African marathoners, contributing to the continent's domination of this distance in the decades that followed.

The 1964 Tokyo Marathon remains a legendary performance, not only for Bikila's impressive time, but also for the way he overcame adversity and pushed back the limits of human endurance. His feat left a lasting imprint on the history of athletics, symbolizing determination, mental strength and self-mastery under the most demanding conditions.

Fact 29 - Olympic champions' training techniques

Olympic track and field champions are not just natural talents: they have to follow rigorous and specific training techniques to reach the highest level. One of the keys to their success lies in meticulous physical preparation, which combines cardiovascular training, strength training and discipline-specific exercises. Each session is designed to enhance strength, endurance and speed. For example, a sprinter like Usain Bolt would train with repeated 200-meter sprints, to work not only on his speed, but also his ability to maintain that speed over longer distances.

Fractional training is a method widely used by long-distance runners and sprinters. This type of training alternates between periods of intense effort and phases of active recovery. The aim is to push the athlete to reach his or her maximum while gradually increasing his or her capacity to sustain the effort. Mo Farah, champion of the 5,000 and 10,000 meters, often attributed much of his success to split training, which enabled him to build both endurance and speed in the decisive final laps of a race.

Mental preparation is another fundamental pillar of training for Olympic champions. Many top athletes, like decathlete Ashton Eaton, focus on visualization before their events. This technique involves imagining each stage of the competition with absolute precision, preparing their minds to execute each movement perfectly. This visualization, combined with relaxation and stress management sessions, enables them to remain calm and focused even under the intense pressure of the Olympic Games.

Training at altitude is also a technique favoured by marathon and middle-distance champions. By training at altitudes above 2,000 metres, athletes force their bodies to adapt to an environment where oxygen is scarcer. This stimulates the production of red blood cells, improving their ability to transport oxygen to the muscles. Athletes like Olympic marathon champion Eliud Kipchoge often train in mountainous regions of Kenya to take advantage of this physiological advantage.

Finally, one of the special features of top-level athletes is their ability to tailor their training to their body's specific needs. Champions work with trainers, nutritionists and physiotherapists to adapt their program and avoid injury.

Fact 30 - The mystery of ultra-fast sprint starts

The start of a sprint race is one of the most critical moments. In a fraction of a second, sprinters must explode out of the starting blocks with incredible power and speed. But how do some athletes manage to start so quickly that they almost seem to anticipate the gun? The mystery of ultra-fast starts in sprinting lies in a combination of sharp reflexes, perfect technique and methodical training.

Elite sprinters like Usain Bolt and Maurice Greene don't just run fast. They work intensively on their reaction at the start. In fact, from the moment the gun goes off, every millisecond counts. The best sprinters have reaction times of around 0.15 to 0.18 seconds, close to the human physiological limit. This allows them to propel themselves even before their brains have fully registered the sound signal, a phenomenon which often leads people to think that these athletes are anticipating the start, when in fact it's an instinctive response.

Technique also plays a crucial role in the speed of the start. Athletes spend hours perfecting their position in the starting blocks, a key element in maximizing the initial explosion. Body position, leg angle and trunk inclination are meticulously adjusted to ensure that all muscular power is transferred into the first burst. A sprinter like Justin Gatlin, for example, is renowned for his explosive start, often considered one of the fastest in the world thanks to his rigorously honed technique.

Another important factor in ultra-fast starts is training the muscles to react at lightning speed. Plyometric exercises, which develop muscle power through explosive movements such as jumps and short accelerations, are at the heart of sprinters' preparation. This type of training strengthens not only the speed of the legs, but also the coordination needed to launch the body forward from the first heel strike against the ground.

Finally, mental concentration is essential for a perfect start. Olympic sprinters spend hours repeating the same movements and visualizing their start, so that the gesture becomes almost automatic. This mental preparation enables athletes to reduce the response time between the start signal and their first push off the blocks. An excellent example of this is Florence Griffith-Joyner, whose legendary starts were the fruit of extraordinary mental focus.

Fact 31 - The first 10,000m record on TV

On June 20, 1949, a historic event in sport took place when the first 10,000-meter world record was broadcast on television. This legendary race took place at an athletics meeting in Helsinki, Finland, and the hero of the day was Finnish runner Viljo Heino. In front of thousands of television viewers, Heino broke his own world record by crossing the finish line in an impressive time of 29 minutes and 27.2 seconds.

This moment was important not only in terms of sporting performance, but also for the evolution of media coverage of sporting events. For the first time, the general public was able to follow an endurance race of this scale live, marking a new era in the way athletics competitions were shared with the world. Thanks to television broadcasts, the athletes' exploits could now inspire and fascinate millions of people, far beyond the spectators in the stadium.

Heino, already an emblematic figure in Finnish athletics, ran this race with a perfectly mastered strategy. Known for his stamina and ability to maintain a high pace for long periods, he ran an intelligent race, controlling each lap with precision. His performance showed not only his great physical fitness, but also his ability to handle the pressure of a historic event broadcast live on television for the first time.

The broadcast of this race also allowed the world to discover the 10,000 metres in a new light. While many considered this event long and less exciting than sprint races, Heino's steady pace and world record captured the public's attention and demonstrated the beauty and complexity of endurance. Television offered a window into the details of performance, physical exertion and tactical race management, revealing a new level of depth in the sport.

This event marked a turning point in the way athletics competitions were perceived and followed. Viljo Heino's performance, immortalized on television, remains a historic moment, not only for the world of athletics, but also for the way sport is shared with the public. It paved the way for the growing popularity of athletics on television, and made legendary moments accessible to generations of fans around the world.

Fact 32 - How altitude affects runners' performance

Altitude has a major impact on runners' performance, as it directly modifies the amount of oxygen available in the air. As altitude increases, atmospheric pressure decreases, meaning that the air contains less oxygen. This makes breathing more difficult for athletes, particularly long-distance runners, who depend on a constant supply of oxygen to sustain their effort. Yet this difficulty can also be turned into an advantage for those who train regularly in these conditions.

Runners training at high altitude develop a unique capacity for adaptation. Their bodies produce more red blood cells to compensate for the lack of oxygen. These cells carry more oxygen to the muscles, improving endurance once back down to sea level. Athletes like Eliud Kipchoge, multiple marathon champion, regularly train in mountainous areas, particularly in Kenya, where altitudes exceed 2,000 meters. This training method strengthens their lung and cardiovascular capacity.

However, not all types of racing benefit equally from altitude. For sprinters and jumpers, the thinner air at high altitude can be an advantage. At the 1968 Olympic Games in Mexico City, held at an altitude of 2,240 metres, world records were broken in the sprint and long jump. The lighter air creates less resistance, enabling runners to reach higher speeds and jumpers to throw themselves farther. This was the case for Bob Beamon, who achieved his legendary 8.90-meter jump in these conditions.

On the other hand, for long-distance races such as the marathon, performance at high altitude can be compromised. Prolonged exertion in oxygen-depleted air forces runners to adjust their pace to avoid exhaustion. Even the most seasoned runners need to be cautious and prepare their bodies well to avoid problems such as altitude sickness or rapid exhaustion, especially in environments where oxygen is significantly reduced.

Altitude training has thus become an indispensable method for elite runners, although altitude itself also poses challenges. For athletes, it's a question of adaptation: if they master these extreme conditions, they can come back stronger and more successful in competitions at sea level, turning the obstacle of altitude into a competitive advantage.

Fact 33 - Athletes who ran despite serious injuries

Athletics is a sport that demands extreme physical endurance, and some athletes have made history by continuing to run despite serious injury. One of the most poignant examples is that of British runner Derek Redmond at the 1992 Barcelona Olympic Games. During the semi-final of the 400-meter race, while in the thick of the race for a place in the final, Redmond seriously injured his Achilles tendon midway through the race. Despite the unbearable pain, he refused to give up. Supported by his father, who came down from the stands to help him, Redmond finished the race to the applause of the audience, in a scene that has become symbolic of courage and perseverance.

Another famous example is that of Gabriela Andersen-Schiess, a Swiss marathon runner who took part in the 1984 Los Angeles Olympic Games. During the first women's Olympic marathon, Gabriela suffered heatstroke and severe cramps in the final kilometers. Although disoriented and exhausted, she refused to leave the race and staggered to the last few meters, watched by concerned spectators and officials. Her arrival at the finish line, though far from the front-runners, made a lasting impression thanks to her determination and refusal to give up despite her suffering.

Athletics is full of stories of athletes' willpower overcoming the physical limits of their bodies. At the 2012 London Olympics, Manteo Mitchell, an American runner, literally finished a race with a fractured fibula. In the middle of a 4x400-meter relay, he felt intense pain after hearing a crack in his leg. Despite this, he continued to run the last 200 meters, securing his team a place in the final. Mitchell later explained that he didn't want to let his teammates down, even at the cost of a serious injury.

These examples show that the mental strength of these athletes is as impressive as their physical ability. Serious injuries have not prevented them from continuing to fight their way to the finish line. While these situations may sometimes seem reckless, they illustrate the spirit of self-sacrifice and self-transcendence that is the hallmark of athletics.

These moments of heroism often have more symbolic value than the victories themselves. They remind us that in sport, as in life, true triumph sometimes lies in perseverance in the face of adversity, and that even in defeat, there are victories of character to celebrate.

Fact 34 - The hottest marathon in Olympic history

The marathon at the 1964 Tokyo Olympic Games is remembered as one of the most grueling, largely due to the intense heat that prevailed that day. Temperatures reached over 30 degrees Celsius with high humidity, turning this already difficult event into a real test of survival for the runners. The athletes had to cope with extreme conditions that day, which had a considerable impact on their performance and endurance.

Ethiopia's Abebe Bikila, already Olympic champion in Rome in 1960, once again proved his dominance in this event, winning the gold medal. Bikila, known for his incredible stamina, overcame the sweltering Tokyo heat with impressive mastery. Not only did he win the race, he did so by breaking the world record with a time of 2 hours, 12 minutes and 11 seconds, becoming the first man to win two consecutive Olympic marathons.

Conditions were so extreme that several runners were unable to finish the race, suffering from dehydration and exhaustion. The organizers had taken precautions by increasing the number of hydration points along the route, but despite this, the heat slowed down the majority of participants considerably. Experts at the time had rarely seen such a physically demanding race, where the impact of weather conditions had so much influence on the final result.

Bikila, who had undergone appendicitis surgery only a few weeks before the race, impressed with his strategy. Known for his ability to remain calm under pressure, he ran methodically, maintaining a steady pace without letting the heat affect him. Unlike many of his rivals, who attempted faster starts and then suffered from the conditions, Bikila accelerated at the right moment, gradually distancing his opponents over the final kilometers.

The 1964 Tokyo Marathon remains an example of the ability of athletes to overcome extreme conditions. Not only did Abebe Bikila break records, he also proved that managing heat and effort is just as crucial as pure speed in endurance races. This moment remains engraved in the history of the Olympic Games and in marathon legend.

Fact 35 - Old and new athletics facilities

Athletes' equipment has evolved radically over the decades, contributing directly to the record performances we see today. At the beginning of the 20th century, running shoes were very rudimentary: leather soles that were studded, heavy and not very flexible. Athletes of the time had to contend with equipment that restricted their movements and made racing more difficult. For example, at the 1936 Olympic Games, Jesse Owens wore leather shoes with simple studs under the sole to improve grip.

Today's running shoes are concentrates of technology. Brands such as Nike and Adidas have developed ultralight shoes, with soles designed to optimize energy return with every stride. Materials such as carbon and reactive foam have revolutionized performance, particularly in long-distance and marathon running. Current world records in sprints and marathons are partly attributed to these innovations, which reduce fatigue and increase propulsion.

The tracks themselves have changed a great deal. Originally, they were made of ash or clay, offering little stability to runners. In 1968, at the Mexico Games, the first tartan track was used, a synthetic surface that enabled athletes to run faster while reducing the risk of injury. This surface, still in use today, has optimized runners' performance by providing better grip and absorbing some of the impact. The difference is such that comparing performance on old and new tracks has become almost impossible.

Throwing equipment, such as javelins and hammers, has also evolved. For example, in the 1950s, javelins were made of wood or simple metal, which limited precision and distance. Today, javelins are made from composite materials, which are lighter and more aerodynamic, enabling longer, more stable throws. Moreover, throwing techniques have evolved in parallel with these innovations, maximizing athletes' efficiency.

Even athletes' clothing has undergone a major transformation. Once made from heavy cotton, modern athletic outfits are made from technical materials that wick away perspiration, reduce friction and provide better ventilation. It may seem trivial, but the comfort provided by these innovations plays a key role in an athlete's ability to stay focused and perform at his or her best during a competition.

Fact 36 - The world's largest athletics stadium

The world's largest athletics stadium is the May Day Stadium in Pyongyang, North Korea. Built in 1989, this colossal stadium can accommodate up to 114,000 spectators, making it not only the largest for athletics, but also one of the largest sports complexes ever built. Located on Rungnado Island, the stadium takes its name from International Labour Day, celebrated on May 1st, and is used for large-scale sporting events as well as political demonstrations.

What sets this stadium apart, apart from its impressive size, is its unique architecture. Its petal-shaped roof evokes a flower in full bloom, covering a large part of the stands and offering a visual spectacle as grandiose as it is functional. In addition to athletics competitions, the May Day Stadium has hosted numerous artistic and cultural events, such as the famous Arirang Festival, a mass gymnastics show in which thousands of participants perform synchronized choreography.

In terms of athletics, although the May Day Stadium is not used for regular international competitions such as the Olympic Games or World Championships, it remains an iconic venue for sporting events in North Korea. Its huge athletics track meets international standards, and the stadium is equipped to host a wide variety of events, from sprint races to jumping and throwing events.

The stadium was renovated in 2014 to improve its facilities and modernize its infrastructure. With a capacity far exceeding that of most stadiums in the world, it represents a symbol of grandeur for the country, but also a place where athletics can be celebrated on a spectacular scale. On the rare occasions when athletics competitions are held there, the grandeur of the venue attracts particular attention.

Although other stadiums such as London's Olympic Stadium or Beijing's National Stadium are more often associated with major athletics competitions, the May Day Stadium remains, in terms of capacity, the largest in the world. It is a reminder of the extent to which athletics can be part of monumental projects, testifying to the symbolic importance that sport can take on in diverse cultural and political contexts.

Fact 37 - Athletes who competed in several disciplines

Some track and field athletes have made history by mastering not one, but several disciplines. One of the most famous examples is American Jim Thorpe, considered one of the greatest athletes of the 20th century. At the 1912 Olympic Games in Stockholm, Thorpe won two gold medals, one in the pentathlon and the other in the decathlon, two extremely demanding events combining running, jumping and throwing. His incredible versatility led to him being hailed as "the world's greatest athlete" by the King of Sweden at the time.

Other athletes, such as Jackie Joyner-Kersee, have also shone in several disciplines. Joyner-Kersee is widely recognized for her exploits in the heptathlon and long jump. At the 1988 Olympic Games in Seoul, she not only won gold in the heptathlon, but also the gold medal in the long jump. Her dominance in both events shows just how exceptional her physical strength, endurance and technique were. Joyner-Kersee was also the first woman to surpass 7,000 points in the heptathlon, a rare feat even today.

Daley Thompson, a British athlete, is another great name who has left his mark on athletics, competing in several disciplines. A decathlon specialist, he won Olympic gold in 1980 and 1984, becoming one of the few athletes to successfully defend his title in this complex event. The decathlon requires mastery of sprinting, throwing and jumping events, as well as long-distance running, making Thompson a model of versatility.

This kind of versatility is not limited to combined events such as the decathlon or heptathlon. Some athletes distinguish themselves by excelling in very different disciplines. For example, Carl Lewis, one of the greatest sprinters of all time, also excelled in the long jump, winning four Olympic gold medals in this event, in addition to his sprint titles. His ability to compete at an elite level in two very different disciplines shows an incredible mastery of his body and techniques.

These versatile athletes demonstrate that specialization in a single discipline is not the only path to excellence in athletics. Their ability to dominate multiple events is a testament to their incredible talent, determination and rigor. They remain a source of inspiration for athletes the world over, showing that versatility and mastery of several disciplines can lead to the pinnacle of world sport.

Fact 38 - The first women's Olympic marathon in 1984

In 1984, at the Los Angeles Olympic Games, the women's marathon was run for the first time, marking a major breakthrough for women in the world of athletics. For a long time, Olympic organizers believed that women were not capable of running such long distances. This preconception was finally shattered, and women were able to prove their incredible endurance and resilience. The first women's Olympic marathon was won by American Joan Benoit, who ran a memorable race.

Joan Benoit finished the race with an impressive time of 2 hours, 24 minutes and 52 seconds. Benoit, known for her fast and daring running style, took the lead from the very first kilometers, leaving renowned competitors such as Norwegian world champion Grete Waitz behind. Her victory was all the more impressive given that she had just recovered from knee surgery a few weeks prior to the Games.

This 1984 marathon not only changed the perception of women in long-distance running, but also paved the way for many other athletes. The race took place in the Californian heat, an added challenge for the women runners, but it didn't dampen their determination. The images of Benoit entering the stadium alone, cheered on by thousands of spectators, made Olympic history.

Another memorable moment of the race was the dramatic finish of Switzerland's Gabriela Andersen-Schiess. Exhausted and dehydrated, she staggered into the final meters, refusing to give up despite her physical condition. Although she finished well behind Benoit, her courage and perseverance left a lasting imprint on the history of women's marathon running, proving that the spirit of competition goes beyond victory.

The introduction of the women's marathon at the 1984 Olympic Games marked a turning point for women in athletics, opening doors to new generations of athletes and permanently changing the way women were perceived in top-level sport. Joan Benoit and her competitors not only ran for themselves, but for all the women who had been excluded from these events for so many years.

Fact 39 - The longest winning streaks in athletics

In the history of athletics, few athletes have managed to dominate their discipline for as long as Edwin Moses. A specialist in the 400-metre hurdles, Moses won 122 consecutive races between 1977 and 1987, an entire decade without defeat. His technical mastery of the hurdles, his methodical preparation and his ability to maintain an incredibly consistent pace made him an athletics legend. Edwin Moses became the symbol of consistency and perfection, dominating the event at a time when competition was fierce.

In the long-distance races, another historic domination is that of Haile Gebrselassie. The Ethiopian runner crushed the world stage in the 10,000 meters during the late 1990s and early 2000s. He won back-to-back Olympic titles in 1996 and 2000, and also won several world championships. Known for his light stride and ability to accelerate in the final laps, Gebrselassie maintained an almost unrivalled supremacy over this distance, creating an impression of total domination.

In the sprint events, Carl Lewis dominated the long jump for almost 10 years, winning four Olympic gold medals in this discipline between 1984 and 1996. Although he is best known for his success in sprinting, it is his longevity in the long jump that remains impressive. Lewis also won 65 consecutive long jump victories, a remarkable run that cemented his place among the greatest athletes of all time.

Women's athletics are no exception. In the 1980s and 1990s, Jamaican sprinter Merlene Ottey dominated the 100- and 200-meter sprint events with remarkable consistency. Although she was often a silver or bronze medallist at the Olympic Games, she maintained an impressive string of victories in world competitions, including world championships and international meetings. Her longevity, spanning more than 40 years, has made her an icon of world athletics.

These exceptional series of victories testify to the rarity of such performances. Maintaining a level of excellence over a long period of time, in the face of global competition, requires not only natural talent, but also iron discipline, rigorous preparation and mental toughness. Athletes such as Edwin Moses, Haile Gebrselassie and Carl Lewis have forever marked the history of their sport, becoming models of excellence and perseverance for future generations.

Fact 40 - The incredible long jump techniques of the 90s

The 1990s marked a revolution in long jumping, with the emergence of highly sophisticated jumping techniques that enabled athletes to push back the boundaries of the discipline. One of the most striking moments of this era was Mike Powell's world record jump at the 1991 Tokyo World Championships. With an incredible jump of 8.95 meters, Powell beat Bob Beamon's legendary record from 1968. To this day, it remains one of the longest jumps ever recorded.

What sets this era apart is the technical precision that athletes brought to every phase of the jump. There's more to the long jump than just the run-up and take-off. The run-up of the athletes of the 90s, for example, was carefully calculated to allow maximum acceleration while maintaining perfect speed control. Mike Powell, like Carl Lewis, known for his mastery of the long jump, used a millimetric running cadence to maximize the efficiency of the last step before the impulse.

The impulse itself has also been perfected. Jumpers in the '90s used a technique known as "hitch-kick" or "reel", in which the legs moved in the air to maintain stability and extend flight time. This technique, though complex, helped to regulate the body's trajectory in mid-flight and prevent the feet from falling too soon into the sand. Carl Lewis, who won four consecutive Olympic gold medals in the long jump, mastered this technique perfectly.

In addition to the hitch-kick technique, some jumpers also used the "bunched jump", another technique consisting of bringing the knees up to the chest in mid-air to increase the distance covered. By combining explosive strength and body control, these athletes managed to lengthen their jumps while staying within the confines of the runway.

The 90s also saw an epic rivalry between Carl Lewis and Mike Powell, which captivated the world of athletics. During their duel in Tokyo in 1991, Lewis jumped 8.91 meters, an extraordinary jump that would have been a world record had it not been immediately surpassed by Powell. This competition between the two men symbolized not only sporting excellence, but also the technical evolution of the long jump, where every detail, every physical or technical adjustment could make the difference.

Thanks to these innovations, the jumpers of the 90s left an indelible mark on athletics.

Fact 41 - The surprising origin of the relay race

The relay race, so common today in athletics competitions, has a much more ancient and surprising origin. This event has its roots in the messengers of antiquity, particularly in Greek civilization. In those days, messengers ran long distances to convey important, often military, messages. These races were literally life-or-death relays, where a stick (or skytalos in Greek) was passed from one runner to another to ensure rapid transmission of information.

The idea of passing on a baton, which today has become the famous témoin, is therefore a direct legacy of these ancestral races. This symbolic gesture represents the passing of responsibility and speed between athletes. Over time, this practice evolved, first becoming a ceremonial ritual before gradually integrating the world of modern sport, where it is now a flagship event in international competitions. The Greeks themselves organized relay races during certain religious festivities, such as the Panathenaic Games, when sacred fire was carried from one temple to another.

It wasn't until the early 20th century that the relay race as we know it today made its Olympic debut. In 1908, at the London Games, the 4x400-meter relay race was officially introduced into the Olympic program. The event quickly gained in popularity, largely due to the excitement it generates with its rapid changes of pace and the crucial importance of coordination between team members.

Another fascinating aspect of relay racing is the importance of the baton itself. This simple, light, cylindrical object is at the heart of the event. Passing the baton is one of the most critical moments in the race. A bad exchange can wipe out a team's chances, even if they're the fastest the rest of the way. Legendary teams such as the Jamaican relay, featuring runners like Usain Bolt, have shown just how decisive the effective handover is in securing victory.

In this way, the relay race embodies much more than mere speed. It symbolizes the coordination, confidence and heritage of the runners of yesteryear, whose lives sometimes depended on these relays. Today, this event is one of the most spectacular in athletics, skilfully blending tradition and modern performance, while recalling the age-old history of the rapid transmission of a message from one runner to the next.

Fact 42 - 400m hurdles speed records

The 400-meter hurdles is one of the most demanding events in athletics, combining speed, endurance and technique. The athlete must complete a full lap of the track, clearing ten hurdles at regular intervals. The current men's world record holder is Karsten Warholm, who stunned the world in 2021 with an incredible time of 45.94 seconds at the Tokyo Olympics. This record was described as a "perfect race" and marked a new milestone in the history of this discipline.

Before Warholm, the 400-meter hurdles record had already been raised to incredible heights by athletes such as Edwin Moses. Moses, a true athletics legend, dominated the discipline in the 1970s and 1980s, remaining unbeaten for 122 consecutive races and setting several world records. His best time of 47.02 seconds, set in 1983, remained unbeaten for 9 years. Moses combined a perfectly synchronized stride with an exceptionally precise hurdling technique, enabling him to run at a constant speed while clearing obstacles with ease.

On the women's side, Sydney McLaughlin also redefined the limits of the discipline in 2021, breaking the world record with an extraordinary time of 51.46 seconds at the Tokyo Olympics. Her race is remembered for its explosive power and perfect handling of the hurdles. McLaughlin, aged just 21, combined blistering speed with exceptional hurdling technique to shatter the previous record held by her compatriot Dalilah Muhammad.

The 400-meter hurdles demands a unique combination of athletic qualities: the ability to maintain high speed while clearing the hurdles without slowing down is what distinguishes the best in this event. Coordination between stride and hurdle height is essential. For example, a change of pace or stride at the wrong moment can throw the athlete off balance and ruin his chances of victory. This mastery of rhythm and technique was crucial in the records set by Warholm and McLaughlin.

Speed records in the 400-meter hurdles continue to evolve, with athletes pushing ever further the limits of what was thought physically possible. Thanks to advances in training techniques, stride optimization and faultless mental preparation, performances in this discipline continue to impress, regularly redefining the standards of athletic excellence.

Fact 43 - The champions who defied age and stayed on top

Athletics is often associated with youth and vitality, but some champions have proved that age is no barrier to staying at the top of their sport. One of the most emblematic examples is Jamaican sprinter Merlene Ottey. After starting her international career in the 1980s, she continued to compete at elite level until she was 50. Ottey competed in seven Olympic Games and won nine Olympic medals, a rare feat that testifies to her exceptional longevity in the world of sprinting.

Another legendary figure is Carl Lewis, who, although best known for his successes in the 1980s, continued to dominate long jumping until the late 1990s. At the age of 35, he won his fourth consecutive long jump gold medal at the 1996 Olympic Games in Atlanta, defying expectations as to the optimum age for athletes in his discipline. Lewis has shown that experience, combined with rigorous training, can keep an athlete at the top, even when many consider it time to retire.

In the marathon, Haile Gebrselassie's example is equally impressive. Although he dominated long-distance events in the 1990s and 2000s, Gebrselassie continued to break records after he passed the age of 35. He bettered his own marathon world record at the age of 35 with a time of 2 hours 3 minutes 59 seconds at the Berlin Marathon in 2008. His perseverance and ability to remain competitive despite the wear and tear of time make him one of the greatest athletes of all time.

Among throwers, American Gail Devers has remained successful in international competitions well into her 30s. A specialist in the 100-meter hurdles, she won three Olympic gold medals over the course of her career and continued to race in world competitions well into her 40s. Devers, who was often plagued by injury, bounced back with unrivalled training rigour and sheer determination, proving that age can never limit dreams of excellence.

These athletes show that mental and physical endurance can push back the limits imposed by aging. Thanks to their discipline, passion and ability to adapt to changes in their bodies, they have not only broken records, but also prejudices about age in sport. They inspire generations of athletes to believe that a sporting career doesn't have to end when the first wrinkles appear, and that dreams of victory are always possible, whatever your age.

Fact 44 - How shot put became a key discipline

Shot-putting, now considered one of track and field's flagship events, dates back to ancient times, when men competed by throwing heavy objects to demonstrate their strength. It was only at the end of the 19th century that this discipline was structured and integrated into modern competitions, notably with the first Olympic Games in 1896. Shot put has been part of athletics since the very beginning of the modern era, symbolizing raw power and technical mastery.

In the early days, athletes used the so-called "gliding" technique, which consisted in making an explosive thrust after gliding along the launch circle. This method was effective, but limited in terms of distance. It wasn't until 1951 that Parry O'Brien, an American athlete, revolutionized shot put by introducing the "rotary" technique. This technique involved spinning around to generate more centrifugal force, enabling the shot put to be thrown at much greater distances. Thanks to this innovation, O'Brien won two Olympic gold medals and broke world records on several occasions.

The evolution of the discipline has also been marked by iconic figures such as Randy Barnes, who still holds the men's world record with a throw of 23.12 metres in 1990. His performance, the result of intensive training and the optimization of his rotational technique, confirmed the importance of shot put in the world of athletics. On the women's side, Germany's Ilona Slupianek also left a lasting impression in the 1980s, setting records and dominating international competitions.

What makes shot put so fascinating is the combination of brute strength and precise technique it demands. Not only must an athlete be able to generate considerable power with his or her body, but he or she must also master his or her movements perfectly to control the trajectory of the shot put. The final impulse, the position of the feet, the rotation of the torso and the release must be perfectly synchronized to maximize the distance of the throw. This technical complexity makes it an impressive event to watch, and a key discipline in athletics competitions.

Today, the shot put is a mainstay of the Olympic Games and World Athletics Championships. It embodies both the evolution of sporting techniques and the physical excellence of athletes. Its importance in competitions shows the extent to which this discipline, once a simple demonstration of strength, has become a veritable science of movement and performance.

Fact 45 - The fastest races in the rain

Running in the rain is an added challenge for athletes, who not only have to cope with the fatigue and pressure of competition, but also with slippery tracks and reduced visibility. Yet some of the most memorable and fastest races in history have been run in impressive downpours. At the 1993 World Championships in Stuttgart, British runner Colin Jackson broke the world record in the 110-meter hurdles with a blistering time of 12.91 seconds, despite torrential rain. This record remained unbroken for over a decade, underlining Jackson's incredible performance in less than ideal conditions.

Another spectacular example is the 4x100-meter relay race at the 2008 Beijing Olympics, where the Jamaican team, led by Usain Bolt, shattered the world record in light rain. The final time of 37.10 seconds proved that even difficult weather conditions couldn't hold back these athletes' incredible performances. This relay remains one of the defining moments in Olympic history, and the rain, far from detracting from the spectacle, added a dramatic touch to the scene.

Rain can also play a psychological role. At the 1968 Olympic Games in Mexico City, Jim Hines ran the 100 meters in 9.95 seconds, becoming the first man to break the 10-second barrier over this distance. Although the weather conditions were rainy during the qualifying heats, Hines kept his cool and used the poor conditions to concentrate even more on his technique. His record stood for 15 years, and this race went down in history as one of his most memorable.

The marathon, already an extremely difficult event, can become even more demanding in the rain. At the 1964 Tokyo Olympic marathon, Ethiopian athlete Abebe Bikila ran in intermittent showers to win his second Olympic gold medal. The victory confirmed his status as a marathon legend, and Bikila proved that weather conditions, however difficult, could not shake his concentration and endurance.

Rain, although it can be perceived as an obstacle, has never prevented athletes from achieving extraordinary performances. On the contrary, it has often added an epic dimension to races, highlighting athletes' ability to adapt and excel in extreme conditions. These races in the rain are a reminder that athletics is as much about mental strength as it is about physical ability.

Fact 46 - The most hotly contested 4x400m relays in history

The 4x400m relay is one of the most exciting races in athletics, often marked by spectacular twists and turns. The races are particularly intense due to the format, where each team must combine speed, endurance and strategy to hope for victory. One of the most legendary 4x400m relays in history took place at the Sydney 2000 Olympic Games, when the American team, led by Michael Johnson, won the gold medal. The duel between Johnson and the Bahamian athlete on the final lap was exceptionally intense, with Johnson maintaining his lead in the final meters to give his team a memorable victory.

Another legendary 4x400m relay dates back to the 1972 Munich Olympic Games. This race remains famous not only for the rivalry between the USA and Kenya, but above all for the heroic effort of Vincent Matthews, who managed to snatch victory for the American team after a hard-fought battle. The relay came down to the final 100 meters, where Matthews showed extraordinary power to cross the finish line first, marking one of the 4x400m relay's greatest performances.

The 1991 World Athletics Championships in Tokyo also featured an unforgettable 4x400m relay. The USA once again dominated this event, with an incredible finish between Antonio Pettigrew and Roger Black of Great Britain. Although Great Britain led for much of the race, Pettigrew put in a stunning performance on the final lap, catching and overtaking Black to give his team another victory.

The women are not to be outdone when it comes to memorable relays. At the 2016 Olympic Games in Rio de Janeiro, the US women's team won gold after a particularly hard-fought race against Jamaica and Great Britain. This relay is remembered for the excellent coordination of the American relay runners and the spectacular comeback of Allyson Felix, one of the best sprinters in history, who made the difference in the final meters, ensuring her team's victory with a perfect relay.

These races show just how unpredictable and exciting the 4x400m relay is. Each leg can turn at any moment, and the combination of individual talent and teamwork makes these moments unique in the history of athletics. The greatest champions, whether American, British or Jamaican, have all experienced epic battles over this distance, leaving a legacy of suspense and spectacular performances.

Fact 47 - The mental preparation techniques of great champions

Mental preparation is one of the most crucial aspects of performance in athletics, and many champions devote as much time to it as they do to their physical training. Great athletes, such as Usain Bolt or Allyson Felix, have shown time and again that mastery of the mind is essential to maintain concentration and manage pressure. One of the key techniques they use is visualization. Before a big race, they mentally imagine themselves running, overcoming obstacles or crossing the finish line, visualizing every detail with precision. This technique boosts confidence and allows the brain to familiarize itself with success before it even happens.

Rituals are also an important part of mental preparation. Many athletes adopt precise routines before a competition, whether it's a specific way of tying their shoes, listening to a particular playlist or rehearsing a gesture. These seemingly innocuous rituals provide a sense of control in an often unpredictable environment. For example, Michael Johnson, famous for his fluid stride and upright posture, always performed a series of specific stretches before running, to ensure that his body and mind were in perfect harmony.

Another common technique is breath management. Endurance athletes, such as marathon runners or long-distance runners, use breathing exercises to calm their heart rate and improve concentration before and during the race. Mo Farah, double Olympic champion in the 5,000 and 10,000 meters, is an adept of this method. By controlling his breathing and concentrating on each inhalation, he manages to remain relaxed even during the most stressful moments of the competition, enabling him to conserve energy and optimize his performance.

Great champions also set themselves clear objectives, not only in terms of victory, but also on how to manage each stage of their race. They focus on specific details at every moment, whether it's the speed to be maintained, body position or breathing rhythm. This focus allows them to avoid distractions, such as the noise of the crowd or the performance of other runners. Carl Lewis, one of the greatest athletes of all time, often spoke of the importance of staying in "one's own bubble" during competition, concentrating only on what one can control.

Finally, mental resilience is what distinguishes great champions from good athletes. After a defeat or setback, they know how to bounce back quickly.

Fact 48 - The closest 200m sprint races

The 200 meters is a unique event, combining the explosive speed of the 100 meters with a technical turn that can change everything. Some of the most memorable races in the history of athletics have taken place over this distance, not least because of the tiny gap separating the runners at the finish line. At the 1968 Olympic Games in Mexico City, the men's 200-meter final was one of the tightest ever. American Tommie Smith won the race with a record time of 19.83 seconds, but the real suspense was behind him, where the other sprinters finished within a whisker of each other. His compatriot John Carlos took third place, but only by a tiny margin from Italy's Pietro Mennea, a duel that will always be remembered for its closeness.

Another spectacular example is the final of the 1991 World Championships in Tokyo. The duel between Michael Johnson and Frankie Fredericks was breathtaking. Johnson, who was already dominating the discipline, had to push the limits of his abilities to maintain a slender lead over the Namibian athlete. The two men were separated by just a few hundredths of a second, Johnson taking victory with a time of 19.79 seconds, while Fredericks came in just behind him.

Women have also delivered memorable duels over this distance. At the Sydney Olympics in 2000, the race between Marion Jones and Pauline Davis-Thompson made history. Jones, the overwhelming favorite, had to fight all the way to the finish to beat Davis-Thompson, who finished just a few hundredths of a second behind. This intense race showed just how much every fraction of a second counts in sprinting, where a wrong stride or a slight imbalance can cost victory.

One of the closest races in the 200-meter sprint remains that of the 2008 Beijing Olympics, when Usain Bolt broke the world record in 19.30 seconds. But behind him, the battle for second place between Churandy Martina and Wallace Spearmon was hotly contested, with Spearmon crossing the line barely a breath behind Martina. However, after the race, disqualifications for going off the line added even more suspense and emotion to an already tense final.

These races show that the 200 metres is an event where the difference between victory and defeat sometimes comes down to details invisible to the naked eye. The stakes are high, and athletes must not only run fast, but also perfectly manage their position in the bend and maintain their speed right to the end. It's this combination of technique and power that makes the 200 metres one of the most spectacular races in athletics.

Fact 49 - The greatest sprinter rivalries in history

Athletics is full of great rivalries, and those between sprinters have always captured the public's attention. One of the most famous rivalries is that between Carl Lewis and Ben Johnson. These two sprinters clashed on several occasions in the 1980s, but it was at the 1988 Olympic Games in Seoul that their duel reached its apogee. Johnson won the gold medal by breaking the world record with a blistering time of 9.79 seconds. However, this triumph was soon marred by a doping scandal, and Lewis reclaimed the medal. Their rivalry made history not only for its impressive performances, but also for its lasting impact on the sport.

Another legendary rivalry is that between Michael Johnson and Donovan Bailey, who dominated the scene in the 1990s. Johnson, a 200- and 400-meter specialist, and Bailey, a 100-meter champion, both ruled their respective distances. Following their victories at the 1996 Olympic Games, a duel to determine the "world's fastest sprinter" was organized in 1997. This race, which combined rivalry and spectacle, did not go as planned, however, with Johnson injuring himself in the middle of the 150-meter race. Their confrontation nevertheless left a strong imprint, underlining the intensity of sprint competitions.

In the 2000s, the rivalry between Usain Bolt and Tyson Gay also captivated the world. Gay, who held several American and world records, was considered one of the best sprinters before Bolt's dramatic arrival on the international scene. Their confrontation at the 2009 Berlin World Championships, where Bolt broke his own world record in 9.58 seconds, marked one of the most iconic moments in sprinting history. Despite Bolt's dominance, Gay never gave up and continued to push his limits to stay in the race.

On the women's side, the rivalry between Florence Griffith-Joyner, better known as Flo-Jo, and Evelyn Ashford in the 1980s left its mark on women's athletics. Ashford, Olympic 100-metre champion, was one of the favourites, but Flo-Jo completely changed the game by setting unrivalled world records in the 100 and 200 metres at the 1988 Olympic Games in Seoul. These two great champions not only pushed the limits of speed, they also showed that rivalry can be a source of inspiration to reach unparalleled heights.

These rivalries have forged the history of sprinting and proved that competition between athletes is often one of the most powerful drivers of sporting excellence.

Fact 50 - The role of coaches in athletes' victories

Behind every great champion there is often a coach whose impact is decisive. These key figures behind the scenes are much more than just technicians. They shape not only the physical performance of their protégés, but also their mentality. One famous example is Glen Mills, Usain Bolt's coach. Thanks to a unique approach combining rigor and freedom, Mills helped Bolt unleash his potential to become the greatest sprinter of all time. He created an environment where Bolt could express his personality while focusing on his performance goals.

Coaches also play an essential role in competition strategy. Bob Kersee, who has coached numerous Olympic champions such as Jackie Joyner-Kersee and Allyson Felix, is renowned for his incredible ability to adapt training to the specific needs of each athlete. He was able to transform Allyson Felix from a talented young athlete into an elite sprinter capable of winning gold medals over several distances. By meticulously analyzing her strengths and weaknesses, Kersee developed a customized training program that has kept Felix at the top of her game for over a decade.

The trainer's role is not limited to physical training. They are also pillars of mental support. Percy Cerutty, coach of Australian athlete Herb Elliott, developed a unique philosophy based on connection with nature and mental willpower. This approach enabled Elliott to remain unbeaten throughout his career in the 1,500 metres and the mile. Cerutty instilled extraordinary mental discipline in his athlete, enabling him to overcome moments of doubt and fatigue.

Coaches must also adapt to evolving techniques and technologies to remain competitive. In the 2000s, Alberto Salazar, coach of famed long-distance runner Mo Farah, used modern recovery techniques, such as hyperbaric chambers and altitude training, to maximize Farah's performance. This innovative approach enabled Farah to win multiple world and Olympic titles in the 5,000 and 10,000 meters. Salazar combines science and traditional training to optimize every aspect of his athlete's performance.

So victories in athletics are never the result of an athlete's talent alone. Behind every success are years of hard work, strategic thinking and moral support from dedicated coaches. Their influence is often discreet, but their contribution is essential to the achievement of the most outstanding feats in the history of athletics.

Fact 51 - The world's most extreme cross-country races

Extreme long-distance races challenge not only the physical limits of athletes, but also their mental endurance. One of the most famous is the Ultra-Trail du Mont-Blanc (UTMB), a 171 km race through the Alps, with over 10,000 meters of ascent. This race, which crosses three countries - France, Italy and Switzerland - exposes runners to unpredictable weather conditions, from summer heat to snowstorms, and demands exceptional effort and fatigue management skills.

The Marathon des Sables, held in the Sahara desert, is another long-distance event renowned for its difficulty. Runners have to cover around 250 km over six days, carrying all their equipment, including food. The extreme climate, with temperatures that can exceed 50 degrees Celsius, and the varied terrain, from dunes to rocky plains, make this competition particularly demanding. It's an event in which managing dehydration, injuries and mental strength are paramount to any hope of reaching the finish line.

The Antarctic Ice Marathon is one of the world's most extreme races due to its environment. Running a marathon on the world's coldest and most inhospitable continent, with temperatures as low as -20 degrees Celsius, requires athletes to be perfectly equipped and prepared to face the cold, the icy wind and the loneliness of the white landscape. This race is a real challenge, where every step is a fight against the elements, much more than against the other participants.

The Badwater Ultramarathon, often described as the world's toughest foot race, takes place in California's Death Valley, in temperatures reaching 55 degrees Celsius. Over a 217 km course, athletes must climb several peaks and manage the extreme heat, making this an event where the slightest error in body management can have serious consequences. It's not uncommon for participants to give up due to the extreme conditions, making every finisher worthy of a feat.

These extreme long-distance races push runners far beyond the simple physical skills required for a classic marathon. They are tests of endurance, mental strength and resilience in the face of often hostile conditions. Athletes competing in these events must not only master their bodies, but also their minds, to overcome challenges that sometimes seem insurmountable.

Fact 52 - The fastest 200m runners in history

The 200 metres is a fascinating event in athletics, combining pure speed and endurance. Athletes must master both an explosive start, technique in the bend, and the ability to maintain maximum speed on the home straight. Among the fastest sprinters in history, Usain Bolt stands out with his incredible world record of 19.19 seconds, set at the 2009 World Championships in Berlin. This phenomenal time, still unbeaten, remains one of the greatest performances ever achieved on the track.

Before the Bolt era, sprinters like Michael Johnson dominated the discipline. In 1996, at the Atlanta Olympic Games, Johnson clocked 19.32 seconds, a record that stood for over 12 years. His unique technique, with a more vertical running style than most of his competitors, enabled him to maintain extraordinary speed throughout the race. This performance is still considered one of the most emblematic moments in modern athletics.

Among women, Florence Griffith-Joyner, nicknamed Flo-Jo, is the fastest 200-meter runner with a world record of 21.34 seconds set in 1988. Her performances revolutionized women's athletics, and her flamboyant style, combined with perfectly mastered technique, made her a sprint icon. Flo-Jo remains a source of inspiration for generations of athletes, her record still standing today.

More recently, athletes like Yohan Blake and Noah Lyles have been pushing the boundaries of the 200 metres. Blake, nicknamed "The Beast", ran 19.26 seconds in 2011, becoming the second-fastest man in history over this distance. As for Lyles, he confirmed his domination of the discipline with a time of 19.31 seconds at the 2022 World Championships, proving that Bolt and Johnson's records continue to inspire new generations.

The 200 metres remains one of the most captivating events on the track and field program. The performances of these sprinters, who seem to defy the laws of physics, testify to the incredible progress of the sport and of human capacities. Whether through their records or their unique running style, these champions have left an indelible mark on the history of athletics.

Fact 53 - The fastest relay races ever recorded

Relay races, where individual speed blends with the precision of baton passing, are among the most exciting events in athletics. In 2012, at the London Olympics, the Jamaican men's team set a dazzling world record in the 4x100-meter relay. Comprising Nesta Carter, Michael Frater, Yohan Blake, and Usain Bolt as the last relay runner, the team finished the race in 36.84 seconds. This time remains unbeatable to this day, combining extraordinary individual performances with smooth baton passing.

On the women's side, the USA hold the 4x100-meter record, also set in London in 2012. The team of Tianna Bartoletta, Allyson Felix, Bianca Knight and Carmelita Jeter crossed the finish line in 40.82 seconds. Their combination of speed, accurate transitions and perfect timing broke a record that had stood for more than 27 years. The U.S. victory that day made women's sprint history.

In the 4x400-meter discipline, the American relays also distinguished themselves. The men's record was set in 1993 by Team USA, with a time of 2:54.29. This record remains unbeaten, with athletes like Michael Johnson running one of the fastest relays in history. Not only is this relay fast, it's also a true test of endurance and effort management over 400 meters.

The women's 4x400-meter relay also sees the USA at the top. The world record, set in 1985 by the Soviet team with a time of 3:15.17, remains a remarkable feat. Yet the performances of American teams at the Olympic Games and World Championships, with runners like Allyson Felix, have consistently approached this mark.

These relay races reveal much more than speed records: they show the importance of teamwork, perfect coordination and the ability to excel under pressure. Each runner relies not only on his or her own performance, but also on the precision of the baton handover, where the difference between victory and defeat can sometimes be decisive.

Fact 54 - Women's 800m world records

The women's 800 metres is one of the most fascinating races in athletics, requiring both speed and endurance. The current world record is held by the Czech Jarmila Kratochvílová, who set a time of 1:53.28 on July 26, 1983 in Munich. This record, which has stood for over three decades, is one of the oldest and most enduring in the history of athletics. Kratochvílová's performance, achieved against a backdrop of Soviet domination in athletics, is remembered for its almost unattainable nature.

The 800-meter race is demanding in many ways. Unlike shorter distances such as the 400 metres, athletes have to manage muscular and respiratory fatigue while maintaining an impressive top speed. Competitors in the 800 metres face a complex strategy: knowing when to accelerate, when to manage their pace, and above all not burning up too much energy in the first lap. Kratochvílová mastered these aspects to perfection, making her record a real feat.

Since the record was set in 1983, many athletes have tried to come close. Runners like South Africa's Caster Semenya have dominated the event over the last decade, with impressive performances flirting with the two-minute mark. However, Kratochvílová's record still seems out of reach, despite advances in training methods and equipment. Semenya, three-time world champion and two-time Olympic champion, made 800m history with a time of 1:54.25 in 2018, the closest to the record in recent years.

It's also an event that demands mental fortitude. The 800 metres is often referred to as a "race of intelligence", where every second counts, and where the slightest mistake can cost victory. Legends such as Maria Mutola, Mozambican Olympic champion in 2000, and more recently Athing Mu, American Olympic champion in 2021, illustrate the evolution of the discipline, but the world record remains as solid as ever.

Kratochvílová's record epitomizes an era, and her longevity in the record books shows how women's athletics has its unavoidable legends. Each new generation of athletes is inspired by this extraordinary feat, an ultimate goal that few dare to dream of achieving.

Fact 55 - The youngest athletes to take part in the Olympic Games

Taking part in the Olympic Games is a dream for many athletes, but some achieve this feat at an age when most children are just discovering the sport. The youngest athlete in Olympic history is Dimitrios Loundras, a Greek gymnast who competed in the 1896 Athens Games at just 10 years of age. In athletics, although rare, a few young prodigies have also made their mark by taking part in this prestigious competition.

In the modern history of the Games, Jamaica's Merlene Ottey qualified for her first Olympic Games in 1980 in Moscow at the age of 20. She went on to become one of the most enduring sprinters, competing in seven consecutive Games. Even younger, however, athletes like American Sydney McLaughlin began their Olympic careers at a very early age. McLaughlin was just 16 when she ran the 400-meter hurdles at the 2016 Rio Games, becoming one of the youngest American athletes to compete in the Olympics.

Another striking example is Chinese sprinter Cheng Yung-chien, who competed in the 1964 Tokyo Olympics at just 15 years of age. Although she didn't win a medal, her participation at this early age shows the level of excellence required to compete at this level. It's rare for such young athletes to reach this stage, as the physical and mental demands of Olympic competition are enormous.

Young athletes' performances at such a prestigious event are a testament not only to their talent, but also to their discipline and resilience. To be able to compete with the best in the world while managing the pressure of representing your country at such a young age is a remarkable feat. These young prodigies often inspire the next generation of athletes, showing them that there is no age limit to reaching for the stars.

Yet the participation of young athletes also raises questions about the impact of such a competition on their physical and mental development. But for those who made their mark at the Games as teenagers, it's proof that talent, when combined with hard work, can reveal itself at an early age.

Fact 56 - The highest pole vault ever!

Pole vaulting is one of the most impressive disciplines in athletics, requiring power, technique and a great deal of courage. Swedish pole vaulter Armand Duplantis holds the record for the highest jump ever achieved. In 2020, he cleared an incredible 6.18 meters, setting a new world record in Toruń, Poland.

Pole vaulting has always fascinated, but what makes Duplantis' feat so special is his youth and rapid progression. Born into a family of pole vaulters, he began practicing the sport at an early age, under the guidance of his father. Duplantis was just 20 years old when he broke the previous record, which was held by Renaud Lavillenie, another pole vaulting great, with 6.16 meters.

This impressive record was not set under ideal conditions. During his jump, Duplantis had to deal with the pressure of major competitions, as well as the mental and physical fatigue that pole vaulters experience when attempting such dizzying heights. Pole vaulting is all about precision: choosing the right pole, adjusting your running speed, and controlling your body in the air.

Historically, this discipline has evolved from the use of bamboo or wooden poles in the early 20th century to the carbon-fiber and glass-fiber poles used today. These modern materials enable athletes to propel themselves to heights previously unthinkable, as demonstrated by Duplantis.

His record is the fruit of many years of rigorous training and technical refinement. Pole vaulting continues to captivate spectators with its daring attempts to defy the laws of gravity, and Duplantis' record is a spectacular example of what humans are capable of achieving with determination and passion.

Fact 57 - Distance records in the triple jump

Triple jump is a fascinating athletic discipline that combines power, technique and coordination. Athletes must perform three distinct impulses, making it an exercise in balance and precision. The men's world record in this event has been held since 1995 by British athlete Jonathan Edwards, with an extraordinary distance of 18.29 meters achieved at the World Championships in Gothenburg, Sweden.

Jonathan Edwards made triple jump history by pushing the limits of what seemed humanly possible. His record-breaking jump was not only impressive for its distance, but also for the consistency of his performance over this period. Prior to this unprecedented performance, Edwards had already cleared 18 metres in previous competitions, but this mark of 18.29 metres cemented his place in athletics history.

On the women's side, the current record is held by Venezuela's Yulimar Rojas, who reached a distance of 15.67 meters in 2021 at the Tokyo Olympic Games. Her phenomenal leap not only broke the Olympic record, but also dethroned the previous world record, which had stood for over 25 years. Rojas' performance testifies to the evolution of this discipline over the decades.

The triple jump is an event that requires explosive speed and total body control in all three phases of the jump: the take-off phase, the stride phase and finally the long jump phase. Precision of movement is essential to maintain speed while maximizing distance. Edwards and Rojas are perfect examples of athletes who have mastered this complex art.

These impressive records remain milestones in the history of the triple jump, and each generation of athletes strives to come close to these performances. Thanks to their perseverance and talent, Edwards and Rojas embody excellence in this demanding discipline, inspiring athletes the world over to take on new challenges.

Fact 58 - Starting techniques that change everything in sprinting

The sprint start is a decisive moment that can make the difference between victory and defeat. It is one of the most technical aspects of the race, where every fraction of a second counts. Professional sprinters spend hours perfecting their starting posture and reaction to the gun. Mastery of the starting blocks is essential, as explosive thrust from the very first steps guarantees a good launch into the race.

Starting blocks have revolutionized sprint performance since their introduction in the 1920s. These tools enable athletes to stabilize their feet to maximize propulsive power from the kick-off. The placement of the feet in the blocks is strategic: some athletes opt for a more aggressive position, with a steeper angle, while others prefer a more conservative angle to better control their balance at the moment of impulse.

One of the great examples of starting technique is Usain Bolt, the fastest man of all time. Paradoxically, Bolt wasn't always the quickest to react to the starting shot. His tall stature made his first steps slower than those of his rivals. However, his incredible acceleration over the last 50 meters more than made up for this slight initial delay. This proves that even an imperfect starting technique can be overcome by other athletic qualities.

Reaction time is also a key factor in sprint starts. Top-level sprinters generally react within 0.15 seconds of the pistol shot. Reacting too quickly, however, can result in disqualification for a false start. Athletes need to find the perfect balance between anticipation and patience to avoid this pitfall, while maintaining maximum explosiveness from the very first step.

With the evolution of technology and training, starting techniques continue to be perfected. Modern athletes analyze their posture, thrust and reaction time with advanced measuring tools to gain those precious hundredths of a second. A good start remains one of the most fascinating and technical elements of sprinting, often decisive in races where victories are decided by a few thousandths.

Fact 59 - The evolution of athletes' uniforms since 1900

Since the beginning of modern competition in the early 20th century, athletes' uniforms have undergone an incredible evolution. In 1900, outfits were heavy and ill-suited to sporting performance. Athletes often wore long pants or baggy shorts, combined with cotton tops that absorbed sweat but weighed down movement. In those days, comfort and aerodynamics were far from priorities.

Over time, the materials used to manufacture these outfits have evolved dramatically. As early as the 1960s, the introduction of synthetic fibers such as nylon changed the game. Lighter, more breathable and able to adapt to the athlete's body, these new fabrics enabled more fluid movements. These innovations coincided with a change in the cut of uniforms, which became more fitted to reduce air resistance.

The arrival of the 80s marked another decisive turning point. Uniforms were now designed not only for comfort, but also to maximize performance. It was at this time that pioneering sports equipment brands began collaborating with athletes to create uniforms using compression technologies. These tight-fitting garments, often made of spandex, help improve blood circulation and reduce muscle fatigue during exercise.

In the 2000s, uniforms became not only a question of performance, but also of aesthetics. Many athletes actively participate in the design of their outfits, adding colors and patterns that reflect their identity. These uniforms are made from ultra-technological materials, sometimes incorporating special microfibers for better thermoregulation and anti-perspirant properties.

Today's athletic uniforms are a concentrate of technology. They are designed to minimize every unnecessary gram and maximize freedom of movement. This evolution shows that an athlete's outfit, once a simple accessory, has become a determining factor in optimizing performance on the track.

Fact 60 - Champions still racing after 40

Age doesn't seem to be an insurmountable limit for some exceptional athletes. Many champions continue to compete and deliver impressive performances well into their 40s. In athletics, while many consider this decade to be the beginning of sporting retirement, athletes like Kim Collins have defied expectations. Collins, a native of St. Kitts and Nevis, ran the 100-meter dash in under 10 seconds at the age of 40, an incredible feat in a discipline where pure speed is often reserved for the very young.

Longevity in athletics is not limited to sprints. Marathon runners such as Spain's Jesús Ángel García have also shown that it is possible to remain competitive with age. García, a race-walking specialist, has taken part in several Olympic Games well into his 40s, maintaining an impressive level of performance despite the physical constraints imposed by this discipline.

These athletes often draw on a level of experience and body management that surpasses that of their younger rivals. Recovery techniques, nutrition and mental preparation play an essential role in these champions' ability to prolong their careers. With better training and competition management, they manage to avoid injury and maintain a high level of fitness.

For many of these athletes, continuing to compete is also a matter of passion. They find competition a source of motivation and a means of pushing back the limits of what is possible. The example of American Bernard Lagat, multiple track and field medalist, is striking. He continued to run long-distance races well into his 40s, proving that technical mastery and mental endurance can rival youth.

These champions are role models for generations to come, showing that with determination and meticulous fitness management, it's possible to defy expectations and stay on top far beyond belief.

Fact 61 - The incredible performances of modern decathletes

Considered one of the most demanding events in athletics, the decathlon comprises ten disciplines requiring strength, endurance and versatility. Modern decathletes have pushed human limits, constantly improving their performance in every event. The discipline includes sprinting, jumping, throwing and long-distance running, testing all athletic abilities in an extremely demanding two-day format.

One of the names that symbolizes this excellence is that of American Ashton Eaton, who dominated the decathlon in the 2010s. In 2015, he broke his own world record with 9045 points, a considerable feat. This score reflects not only outstanding individual performances in every event, but also an ability to maintain a high standard across all ten disciplines. In particular, he achieved performances comparable to specialist sprinters in the 100-meter dash or throwers in the javelin event.

Today's decathletes also benefit from technological advances in equipment and medical monitoring. Training techniques are more precise, using biomechanical data to optimize every movement. This enables them to come even closer to perfection in every event, whether in jumps like the pole vault or throws like the discus. This scientific approach has enabled these athletes to constantly improve their results.

The mental discipline of the decathletes is equally impressive. Over two days of intense effort, physical wear and tear is combined with mental stress. However, the best decathletes manage to maintain extraordinary concentration, managing each event with strategic precision. The sequence of disciplines, in which every detail counts, demands perfect management of energy and mental focus.

The performances of modern decathletes bear witness to the constant evolution of this discipline. They push back the limits of what was once thought possible, proving that the decathlon remains one of the most complete and spectacular events in athletics.

Fact 62 - Relay races on snow-covered tracks

Imagine running a relay on a snow-covered track, where every step is a challenge of balance and precision. It may sound unusual, but relay competitions have been held in these extreme conditions before. Although not common in major official competitions, these events, often held in mountain environments, add an extra challenge for athletes, who must not only run fast, but also adapt to slippery and unpredictable terrain.

Relaying in snowy conditions requires specific skills. Passing the baton, which is already tricky on a standard track, becomes even riskier in the snow. The slightest misstep can result in a fall or loss of balance, requiring perfect synchronization between team-mates. Relay runners also need to adapt their stride to maximize stability, as the slightest error can result in precious seconds being lost, or even jeopardize the entire race.

Taking part in a relay race in the snow requires different mental and physical preparation. Athletes have to work on their balance, flexibility and effort management on harder, more irregular terrain. In addition to conventional training, they have to adapt to these conditions by adjusting their equipment. Shoes with soles adapted to prevent slipping are essential to minimize the risk of falling.

These races offer a unique spectacle for spectators. Seeing athletes battle against the natural elements adds a spectacular dimension to the events, where surpassing oneself depends not only on speed, but also on adapting to climatic conditions. It's also a reminder of the origins of athletics, where running in extreme conditions was part of the sporting adventure.

Despite the difficulty, relays on snow-covered tracks are a real challenge that attracts the most daring athletes. They see it as an opportunity to prove their versatility and show that athletics is not just about stopwatches, but also about resilience in the face of the toughest conditions. These competitions test not only speed, but also mental and physical endurance.

Fact 63 - The greatest feats of high jumpers

The high jump has always fascinated by the grace and power it demands from athletes. One of the most memorable feats is undoubtedly that of Cuban athlete Javier Sotomayor, who set the world record by jumping 2.45 meters in 1993. To this day, this record remains unbeaten, representing the pinnacle of human ability to defy gravity in this discipline.

High jump techniques have evolved over the decades, but the introduction of the "Fosbury flop" in the 1960s marked a decisive turning point. This technique, popularized by American Dick Fosbury at the 1968 Olympic Games, revolutionized the discipline. Instead of crossing the bar from the front or in a scissor, athletes now jump in an arc with their backs to the bar, an approach that maximizes the elevation of the center of gravity.

Other great names have left their mark on this discipline. For example, Stefan Holm, a Swedish athlete, is known for his incredible precision technique and ability to jump well above his own height (1.81 m), reaching heights of over 2.40 m. These performances are impressive, as they show how technique, combined with strength, can take you to unexpected heights.

In the women's competitions, Croatian Blanka Vlašić also dazzled the athletics world. With a personal best of 2.08 metres, she is one of the few female athletes to have broken this mythical barrier. Her performances have left a lasting imprint on the history of this discipline, testifying to the continuing progress of jumpers' physical abilities.

The feats of high jumpers are measured not only in centimetres or metres. They also embody the struggle against human physical limits. Each jump, each attempt, represents a challenge in which the athlete confronts gravity, his or her own body, and sometimes even history.

Fact 64 - The most impressive middle-distance races

Middle-distance races, from 800 m to 1500 m, are among the most exciting in athletics, combining speed, endurance and strategy. One of the most legendary performances in this category came from David Rudisha at the 2012 London Olympics. The Kenyan runner smashed the 800 m world record in 1 minute 40 seconds 91, achieving one of the greatest feats ever seen over this distance.

The 1500 m, often referred to as "the race of kings", also had its moments. Hicham El Guerrouj, the Moroccan nicknamed "King of the 1500 m", still holds the world record with a time of 3 minutes 26 seconds 00, set in 1998. This record has stood the test of several generations of athletes, testifying to the tactical and physical perfection required to excel in this race.

The importance of tactics in these races is often decisive. Runners must not only manage their speed, but also keep an eye on their rivals, particularly in the last 400 m where the battle for victory reaches its climax. In some historic races, such as the 1972 Olympic 800 m final in Munich, American Dave Wottle won the gold medal after a long spell at the back of the pack, before producing a dazzling acceleration in the final meters.

On the women's side, Jarmila Kratochvílová's performance goes down in history. In 1983, she set the world record for the women's 800 m in 1 minute 53 seconds 28, a time still unmatched today. This race marked a turning point in the history of women's middle-distance running, proving that women could achieve unprecedented levels of performance.

Middle-distance races, with their breathless duels and complex strategies, continue to impress spectators. They demand a unique combination of mental strength, explosive speed and effort management, making these events the stuff of legends and memorable feats.

Fact 65 - Running endurance records

Endurance running is a field in which human beings surpass their physical and mental limits. The most emblematic endurance record is undoubtedly that of Yiannis Kouros, nicknamed "the king of ultra-endurance". This Greek athlete has broken several world records in 24-hour and 48-hour races, and over extremely long distances. In 1984, during the New York 24-hour race, he covered a phenomenal distance of 303.506 km, a feat never equalled.

Ultra-marathons, often run over distances of more than 100 km, are a true test of body and mind. Scott Jurek, one of the biggest names in ultra-trail running, has made history by winning such legendary races as the Western States Endurance Run seven times. His victory in the Badwater Ultramarathon, a 217 km race in the extreme heat of Death Valley, is considered one of the most impressive endurance performances ever.

Endurance records also include races in the mountains and over difficult terrain. Kilian Jornet, a Spanish runner, is known for his exploits in trail races. In 2010, he ran the Ultra-Trail du Mont-Blanc, a 171 km race with over 10,000 meters of ascent, in a record time of 20 hours and 36 minutes, an incredible performance that illustrates the power and physical stamina of endurance runners.

Some races, like the Barkley Marathons, reputed to be the toughest race in the world, defy the very notion of human limits. Very few athletes have ever completed it. It takes place in a hostile mountain setting, with a secret course that changes every year, demanding almost inhuman physical and mental endurance.

These endurance records are not only proof of extraordinary physical ability, but also of the mental strength of the athletes. They have to face fatigue, pain, and sometimes extreme weather conditions. These feats demonstrate what human endurance can achieve when mind and body are pushed to their absolute limits.

Fact 66 - The fastest sprinters in the snow

Running in the snow is a rare challenge for sprinters, who are accustomed to tracks in perfect condition. Yet some competitions have seen athletes defy the cold and harsh conditions to set impressive performances. The Winter Olympics do not include sprinting events on snow, but some races in northern climates or special events have seen outstanding performances on snow-covered tracks.

At the Winter Sprint Challenge in Scandinavia, several sprinters stood out for their ability to adapt their technique to slippery terrain. Support becomes unstable, and the crucial start in a sprint has to be adjusted to avoid the risk of a fall. It's in these conditions that athletes like American Jeremy Dodson have shown that it's possible to run fast, even under snow, clocking impressive times despite the inclement weather.

Another striking example occurred at one edition of the Winter University Games in Russia, where the weather conditions took the racers by surprise. The speeds achieved on snow-covered ground, despite a noticeable loss of grip, astonished spectators and officials alike. These races show that even in extreme conditions, the physical and mental preparation of athletes enables them to maintain top-level performances.

The greatest challenge for sprinters in the snow is managing energy and technique. Strides must be shorter and more controlled, while maintaining maximum speed. The ability to maintain good posture and firm footing becomes a real art. This technical adaptation is crucial to maintaining competitiveness in conditions that do not favor pure speed.

So, although snow is not the usual terrain for sprinters, the athletes who took up this challenge proved that even in difficult circumstances it is possible to achieve memorable feats, adding an extra dimension to their endurance and determination.

Fact 67 - Athletics competitions in the middle of a heatwave

Athletics competitions in the middle of a heatwave push athletes to their physical and mental limits. Extreme heat can turn an endurance or sprint event into a real survival challenge. At the Tokyo Olympic Games in 2021, temperatures in excess of 35°C left their mark. Organizers had to reschedule some events to avoid the hottest hours of the day, but that didn't stop the athletes from coping with the scorching heat.

One of the most difficult moments of the competition was the women's marathon. Many athletes had to cope not only with the distance, but also with heatstroke. Some favorites dropped out of the race, exhausted by the extreme conditions. Hydration and effort management strategies took on crucial importance. Additional refreshment stations were set up to allow runners to cool down as much as possible.

In 1983, during the first World Athletics Championships in Helsinki, another historic heat wave hit the events. Record performances were compromised, as the heat affected not only the athletes' physical stamina, but also their concentration. Despite this, several remarkable performances were achieved, underlining the incredible adaptation of these elite athletes' bodies to adverse conditions.

Jumps and throws are also strongly affected by the heatwave. Heat can alter the quality of equipment, for example by making poles softer or surfaces more slippery. What's more, maintaining concentration for hours on end in the blazing sun is as much a mental challenge as a physical one. These competitions have often shown that the preparation of athletes is not limited to their physical condition, but also includes their ability to manage extreme external factors.

Athletics competitions in a heatwave are not only a test of speed and strength, but also of resilience. Every performance achieved in these conditions tells a story of courage and adaptation, essential qualities in a sport where the elements can become as formidable an adversary as any other athlete.

Fact 68 - The crucial role of footwear in Olympic victories

Shoes play a decisive role in Olympic victories, far beyond their simple function of protecting the feet. For decades, footwear manufacturers have been constantly innovating to provide athletes with performance-enhancing equipment. In the 1960s, for example, the first spiked shoes transformed track running. Their design provided better grip and increased propulsion, crucial elements for sprinters.

Over the years, materials have evolved. The leather of the first shoes has given way to ultralight synthetic materials, reducing muscle fatigue over long distances. Midsoles have also been strengthened to provide more cushioning and prevent repeated impact injuries, particularly in long-distance events such as marathons. Athletes such as Eliud Kipchoge, who broke the marathon record, have benefited from shoes equipped with carbon plates to optimize their stride and reduce energy expenditure.

The 2016 Olympic Games in Rio highlighted the impact of these technological advances. Numerous records were broken, particularly in sprinting, where shoes specially designed to promote acceleration over short distances proved their worth. Shoes with strategically positioned spikes enable runners to make the most of their power at the start, the decisive moment in sprinting. The combination of a better fit and discipline-specific materials has enabled athletes to achieve impressive results.

The importance of these shoes is not only linked to speed. In jumping events, such as the high jump or long jump, shoes help optimize impulse during the take-off, a crucial moment for success in these disciplines. For example, the shoes used by Mike Powell for his record-breaking long jump of 8.95 meters in 1991 were designed to maximize stability and flexibility during take-off.

In short, athletics footwear, although often underestimated, has become an essential element of Olympic success. They represent the point of convergence between technology and performance, offering athletes invaluable assistance in their quest for records and medals.

Fact 69 - The most spectacular high jumps ever seen

High jumping is a discipline where technique and power combine to create exceptional moments. One of the most memorable jumps in history is that of Javier Sotomayor, the legendary Cuban high jumper, who cleared 2.45 metres in 1993. This still unsurpassed world record is a symbol of excellence in athletics. Sotomayor, in addition to his imposing stature, had impeccable technique, using the "Fosbury flop" method with unprecedented precision.

This technique, which consists of crossing the bar with one's back to it, was popularized by Dick Fosbury at the 1968 Olympic Games in Mexico City, where he won the gold medal. This innovative style completely revolutionized the discipline, making jumps more spectacular and efficient. Before the introduction of the "Fosbury flop", athletes used more rudimentary techniques, such as the scissor method or the belly roll, but none offered the same potential in terms of height cleared.

In addition to Sotomayor, other athletes have made high jump history with breathtaking performances. Stefan Holm, the Swede, measuring 1.81 meters, cleared impressive heights, reaching 2.40 meters, proving that size isn't everything in this discipline. His meticulous preparation, explosiveness and perfect timing on the take-off made him a formidable jumper, capable of beating bigger and stronger opponents.

Competition conditions can also play a role in the size of these jumps. At the 1980 Moscow Olympics, Italy's Sara Simeoni shone when she jumped 1.97 meters, becoming the first woman to surpass this height in competition. This historic jump ushered in a new era for women in this discipline, inspiring many athletes to aim higher.

In short, the most spectacular high jumps not only pushed back the limits of human performance, but also showed how innovation, technique and determination can transform an already demanding discipline into a true sporting spectacle.

Fact 70 - Incredible photo finish finishes

Photo-finish finishes are moments of rare intensity in athletics, where every fraction of a second counts. One of the most famous examples was at the 1960 Olympic Games in Rome, during the men's 100-meter race. American Armin Hary was declared the winner after unbearable suspense, with a time of 10.2 seconds. Victory came down to a few thousandths of a second, necessitating the use of the photo finish to decide the outcome.

This technology, introduced into athletics competitions from the 1930s onwards, revolutionized the sport. Prior to this, many finishes were judged by eye, which could sometimes lead to errors. The photo-finish captures the precise moment when the first athlete crosses the line, guaranteeing absolute justice in extremely close races. This innovation has become indispensable in disciplines such as the 100 or 200 meters.

At the 2011 World Athletics Championships in Daegu, the 100-meter final once again offered an incredible photo-finish moment. Yohan Blake won the race, taking advantage of a false start by Usain Bolt, but the intensity remained palpable right to the end. Even when the public sees races contested with the naked eye, the use of this technology ensures that the final decision is irrefutable.

The photo finish isn't just for sprint races. In the 1,500-meter race at the 2016 Rio Olympics, American Matthew Centrowitz won gold by a tiny margin. Electronic timing and the photo finish were decisive in deciding between athletes who were so close at the finish.

These spectacular finishes, made possible by technological advances, add a dimension of suspense and fairness to athletics. They remind us that, sometimes, it's a matter of thousandths of a second that separates glory from the rest.

Fact 71 - 1500m world records never broken

The 1500 metres, known as one of the most strategic and demanding distances in athletics, has seen some spectacular records go down in history. Among them, the one set by Hicham El Guerrouj on July 14, 1998 in Rome remains a benchmark. With a breathtaking time of 3:26.00, the Moroccan etched his name in the annals of history. This record is not only a physical feat, but also a tactical masterpiece, highlighting his perfect management of rhythm and power over this distance.

El Guerrouj, often dubbed "the king of the mile", had a unique ability to maintain incredible speeds in the last 400 meters of the race, a decisive asset in this discipline. His record withstood the onslaught of the best runners for over two decades, even in an era when technology and sports science have enabled spectacular improvements in performance in other disciplines.

On the women's side, the current record-holder is Genzebe Dibaba, the Ethiopian who set a new standard in 2015 in Monaco, with a time of 3:50.07. This astounding performance upset the predictions and erased a 22-year-old record held by China's Qu Yunxia. The women's 1500 metres, just as intense as the men's race, has become a field of fierce rivalry, where managing the final sprint often makes the difference.

What makes these records so hard to beat is the balance between endurance, speed and strategy. Every runner needs to know when to accelerate without burning out too early. In a race where the slightest misstep can cost several seconds, these records embody technical and physical perfection. Despite the emergence of young talent, these extraordinary performances remain unattainable for many, testifying to the level of excellence achieved by these champions.

The men's and women's 1500-meter records are milestones that illustrate not only the evolution of middle-distance running, but also the complexity and beauty of this discipline. They are peaks that have yet to be surpassed.

Fact 72 - Athletics competitions in extreme conditions

Athletics, often seen as a discipline that takes place in stadiums with ideal conditions, has also been marked by competitions in extreme environments. One of the most memorable examples is the marathon at the 1968 Olympic Games in Mexico City, run at an altitude of 2,240 meters. The rarefied air considerably affected runners' performance, with faster fatigue and records that seemed unattainable.

Intense heat has also played a decisive role in some competitions. In 1983, the World Athletics Championships in Helsinki saw athletes struggle against stifling heat. Long-distance runners, like marathoners, had to cope with temperatures approaching 30°C, which affected their running strategies and their ability to maintain a steady pace. It's in these conditions that the importance of hydration and effort management takes on its full meaning, as mistakes can lead to abandonment.

Some competitions even took place in torrential rain or strong winds. At the Tokyo 1964 Olympic Games, rain fell on the events, making the track slippery and performances more unpredictable. The long and high jumps suffered particularly badly, with athletes having to adjust their strides and manage the lack of grip on the track.

Competitions on snowy or icy surfaces are rare in athletics, but events such as relays or endurance races have been organized in regions with extreme winter conditions, notably in charity or challenge races. These races require not only physical, but also mental preparation, as the cold can paralyze muscles and slow recovery.

These extreme conditions reveal the resilience and adaptability of athletes. Performing in environments that challenge their physical capabilities, they must adjust their strategies, whether by managing their energy or adopting specific racing techniques. These competitions highlight not only the talents of the champions, but also their ability to overcome natural elements that make them veritable warriors of the slopes.

Fact 73 - The greatest moments in marathon history

The marathon is a legendary athletics event, marked by moments of unique intensity. One of the most famous dates back to the 1908 London Olympic Games, when the official marathon distance was set at 42.195 km. The exhausted Italian runner Dorando Pietri staggered across the finish line, supported by the judges after several falls. Although he was disqualified, this episode etched his name in marathon history and captivated audiences the world over.

In 1960, at the Olympic Games in Rome, Ethiopia's Abebe Bikila made history by winning the gold medal for barefoot running. This legendary performance, under the Arch of Constantine, revealed to the world the talents of African runners, who would later dominate long-distance events. Bikila repeated his feat in Tokyo in 1964, becoming the first athlete to win two consecutive Olympic marathons.

Another unforgettable moment took place at the 1982 Boston Marathon. In a fierce race dubbed "Duel in the Sun", American Dick Beardsley and Briton Alberto Salazar battled it out right up to the last kilometer. In the intense heat, Salazar won by the narrowest of margins, with both riders exhausted by the finish. This confrontation defined the determination and tenacity that characterize marathon runners.

More recently, in 2019, Kenyan athlete Eliud Kipchoge broke a new barrier by running a marathon in under two hours, although this performance was not officially recognized due to unapproved conditions. However, this feat, achieved in Vienna, proved that human limits can still be pushed back, inspiring a whole generation of runners.

The marathon continues to fascinate, not only because of the records it generates, but also because of its human stories, in which effort, surpassing oneself and physical and mental endurance are pushed to extremes. These emblematic moments have forged the legend of the marathon, reminding us that every race is much more than a simple test of speed.

Fact 74 - The secret techniques of elite sprinters

Elite sprinters, often compared to human racing cars, owe their speed not only to their physical qualities, but also to meticulously refined techniques. One of these secrets is absolute mastery of the start phase. A good start is crucial in generating maximum acceleration in the shortest possible time. To achieve this, athletes train with precisely adjusted starting blocks, taking into account their morphology and leg power.

Breathing also plays a decisive role in performance. Contrary to popular belief, sprinters don't necessarily breathe during the race. Some champions hold their breath for most of a 100-meter race, to concentrate all their energy on the explosive effort. This maximizes muscular power while minimizing bodily distractions.

Stride technique is another key element. Sprinters work tirelessly on optimizing the length and frequency of their strides. The aim is to achieve a perfect balance between these two factors, as too long a stride can lead to loss of balance, while too short a stride limits maximum speed. Video sessions are often used to analyze each movement in detail.

The arms, often neglected by amateurs, play an essential role in balance and propulsion. Elite sprinters synchronize their arm movements with their legs to generate extra force and improve stability. Efficient balancing technique can make the difference in a few hundredths of a second, which is crucial at this level.

Finally, recovery is one of sprinters' best-kept secrets. Today's champions invest as much time in recovery as they do in physical training. Cold baths, muscle compression and restful sleep are all part of an overall strategy to keep the body at peak performance race after race. These meticulous details, often invisible to the general public, are the real secrets that transform talented athletes into elite sprinters.

Fact 75 - The most enduring long-distance runners

The most enduring long-distance runners are capable of maintaining an intense pace over distances where both mental and physical endurance are put to the test. Among them are athletes who have made history, such as Haile Gebrselassie and Eliud Kipchoge. Their ability to manage races of several dozen kilometers, while maintaining a sustained pace, is the fruit of rigorous training and iron discipline.

Endurance is a challenge that goes beyond mere physical fitness. These runners have perfect control of their heart rate and breathing, essential skills to avoid burning out too quickly. They also develop precise energy management, balancing moments of relaxation with those of acceleration. Diet and hydration during the race play a crucial role in avoiding the dreaded "fatigue hits", as marathon runners' experience has often shown.

Mental preparation is also a determining factor. Long-distance champions are able to stay focused on their goal for hours on end. They develop a unique ability to overcome pain and fatigue, focusing on visualization techniques and internal mantras. Eliud Kipchoge, for example, is known for his almost meditative calm when running, a state of mind forged by years of experience and training.

Long-distance racing takes place in a wide variety of environments, from urban marathons to extreme mountain events. The champions who excel on these terrains demonstrate impressive adaptability. Kilian Jornet, famous for his ultra-trail exploits, is a perfect example. He has run and won some of the toughest events in the world, where managing external conditions is as important as physical performance.

These runners embody an exceptional form of resistance, where every detail counts: diet, effort management, mental strength. They inspire generations of athletes, not only through their records, but also through their ability to push back the limits of human endurance.

Fact 76 - The most memorable moments of relay races

Relay races, where individual speed is combined with collective coordination, have often provided unforgettable moments in the history of athletics. One of the most striking examples is the 4x100-meter final at the 2008 Olympic Games in Beijing, where the Jamaican team, led by Usain Bolt, not only won gold, but also broke the world record with a breathtaking time of 37.10 seconds. The moment will always be remembered as a demonstration of power and cohesion.

The relay is not just about speed. It also depends on perfect coordination when handing over the baton. A mistake in this crucial phase can wipe out an entire team's efforts, as the American team sadly experienced on several occasions, most notably at the 1995 World Championships, when a botched handover cost them victory. It just goes to show what a test of precision and technical mastery the relay is.

In some races, it's not victory that impresses, but the ability to overcome obstacles. In 1991, at the World Championships in Tokyo, the legendary 4x400-meter relay race made its mark when American Antonio Pettigrew came back strongly on the home straight to overtake his rivals and give his team an unexpected victory. This kind of turnaround highlights the mental strength and perseverance of athletes.

Relay races also have a unique emotional power, as they depend on an entire team. In 2012, the US women's team achieved the feat of breaking a 27-year-old world record in the 4x100 metres at the London Olympics. This moment was a symbol of solidarity and collective work, inspiring generations of young runners to believe in the strength of the team.

Every relay race, whether victorious or not, brings out a form of tension and passion rarely equaled in other disciplines. Whether it's a spectacular comeback, a shattered world record or a last-minute handover, these moments remain etched in the history of athletics, offering lessons in self-transcendence and team spirit.

Fact 77 - The 400m world record never beaten

Wayde van Niekerk's world record in the men's 400 meters at the 2016 Rio Olympics made athletics history. With a time of 43.03 seconds, the South African shattered the previous record held by Michael Johnson since 1999. What makes this feat even more remarkable is that van Niekerk started from lane 8, a position rarely favorable for such a performance. His victory came as a shock to observers and reaffirmed the power and technique needed to master this distance.

The 400 metres is one of the most demanding races, because it's all about finding the perfect balance between pure speed and endurance. Sprinters must maintain an extremely fast pace over a distance which, despite its short appearance, quickly depletes energy reserves. This is what made van Niekerk's performance so historic, as few athletes manage this distance with such efficiency.

This record is all the more impressive when you consider that the 400 metres had already been the subject of several legendary performances in the history of athletics. Runners like Michael Johnson had revolutionized the discipline with their style, pace and race management. But no one expected this record, considered almost unbeatable, to fall that day in Rio, 17 years after it was set.

Wayde van Niekerk stood out not only for his speed, but also for his technical control throughout the race. At the 300-meter mark, when others were slowing down due to fatigue, he accelerated, leaving his rivals behind. It was this ability to maintain maximum speed in the final meters that sealed his place in 400-meter history.

Track and field experts continue to wonder how long this record will stand. With each passing year, new talents emerge, but this time of 43.03 seconds remains an unrivalled benchmark.

Fact 78 - The most powerful javelin throws

Javelin throwing is a discipline in which strength and technique combine to create spectacular performances. Among the athletes who have left their mark on history, Jan Železný is undoubtedly one of the most famous. This Czech athlete still holds the men's world record with a throw of 98.48 meters, achieved in 1996 in Jena, Germany. This record remains unsurpassed, and his throw has become the absolute benchmark in this demanding discipline.

Before Železný, javelin throwing had already seen some impressive performances. The 1980s, in particular, saw several records fall with the introduction of new techniques and advances in the materials used in javelins. However, these technical advances were so significant that the design of javelins had to be modified to prevent them from exceeding the safety limit on stadiums. The javelins flew so far that it became risky for spectators and other athletes.

In the women's category, Barbora Špotáková, also from the Czech Republic, made her mark with a throw of 72.28 metres in 2008. This world record, achieved at the World Cup final in Stuttgart, testifies to her technical mastery and power. Women's javelin throwing has made remarkable progress, and today's athletes are inspired by the exploits of pioneers like Špotáková to push the boundaries ever further.

There's more to javelin throwing than brute force. Technique, speed of execution and coordination between body movements play a crucial role in performance. Athletes spend years perfecting their technique, fine-tuning every detail to maximize the distance covered by the javelin. What's more, weather conditions such as wind can influence performance, making each throw unique.

These spectacular throws continue to inspire new generations of athletes, who dream of surpassing these javelin legends. With the constant evolution of training methods and equipment, it's certain that the javelin throw will continue to produce exceptional moments in the history of athletics.

Fact 79 - Medal-winning athletes with injuries

In the history of athletics, many athletes have defied the odds by winning medals after overcoming serious injuries. These milestones are a testament to the resilience and determination of athletes who refuse to let physical obstacles deprive them of their Olympic dreams. Their ability to get back up despite often intense pain inspires beyond sport.

A famous example is that of British runner Derek Redmond at the 1992 Barcelona Olympics. During the 400-meter semi-final, Redmond collapsed on the track with a torn hamstring. Refusing to give up, he got back up and, supported by his father who had joined him on the track, finished the race to the applause of the crowd. Although he didn't win a medal, this act of courage remains engraved in Olympic history.

Other athletes, such as American sprinter Gail Devers, have also made history by triumphing despite injury. Diagnosed with Graves' disease, an autoimmune disorder that affects the thyroid gland, Devers had to undergo several treatments before returning to competition. Against all odds, she won two Olympic gold medals in the 100-meter dash in 1992 and 1996, proving that an iron will could transcend the body's limitations.

Another inspiring example is that of Jamaican weightlifter and runner Usain Bolt. Despite suffering numerous injuries throughout his career, notably to his hamstring muscles, Bolt continued to dominate the track and became a living legend with multiple gold medals at the Beijing, London and Rio Olympic Games. His blistering speed and injury management impressed the world.

These stories of personal achievement show that it is often the most difficult moments that forge champions. For these athletes, injuries are not the end of the story, but opportunities to rediscover themselves, to rebuild and to continue striving for excellence, despite all adversity.

Fact 80 - The first women to take part in the Olympic Games

The modern Olympic Games, introduced in 1896, were initially reserved for men. However, as early as 1900 in Paris, women were finally able to take part in certain events. This marked a historic turning point, although their possibilities were still limited. For the first time, only 22 women competed in disciplines such as tennis, sailing and even croquet, but athletics was not yet one of their options.

It was at the 1928 Games in Amsterdam that women's athletics were included in the Olympic program for the first time. Events such as the 100-meter, 800-meter and 4x100-meter relays were introduced for women. This event enabled athletes like Betty Robinson, who won the first women's 100-meter gold medal, to make history. She was only 16 at the time, and her triumph caused a sensation in the sporting world.

The inclusion of women in track and field events was not without controversy. The women's 800-meter race, in particular, provoked fierce opposition after a large number of participants collapsed from exhaustion at the finish line. As a result, the event was dropped from the Games until 1960. The event's return showed the growing determination of female athletes to prove their abilities in all disciplines.

Women's place in Olympic athletics evolved gradually, in step with social change. In the decades that followed, more and more disciplines opened up to women, and the number of women taking part increased considerably. These pioneers enabled future generations to push back the boundaries of women's sport.

Today, the Olympic Games offer as many opportunities to women as to men, a result of the struggle and efforts of the first female Olympians. Their achievements paved the way for equality in athletics, and enabled female athletes to establish themselves as icons in the world of sport.

Fact 81 - Athletics champions who defied gravity

Some athletes seem almost to defy the laws of gravity, particularly in disciplines such as long jump and high jump. Bob Beamon, with his legendary jump of 8.90 meters at the 1968 Olympic Games in Mexico City, remains a benchmark in the history of athletics. The jump was so exceptional that it surpassed the previous world record by almost 55 centimetres, leaving the world stunned. This moment, often referred to as the "jump of the century", perfectly illustrates the ability of some to transcend physical limits.

Beamon's impressive performance was no accident. The combination of his explosiveness, his speed and the altitude of Mexico City all contributed to this feat. But it was above all his ability to coordinate all the elements to perfection that made the difference. The long jump requires a technical mastery that goes far beyond the simple run-up and jump: the way the athlete rises, controls his body in the air and lands is crucial to maximizing distance.

In the high jump, athletes like Javier Sotomayor have also pushed the limits. The Cuban still holds the men's world record today, with a jump of 2.45 meters achieved in 1993. The Fosbury flop technique, used to clear the bar, revolutionized this discipline, enabling athletes to use their bodies in a more efficient way to overcome gravity. Prior to this method, jumpers used other techniques, none of which could reach such heights.

Jumps aren't the only area where athletes seem to defy gravity. The performances of triple jumpers such as Jonathan Edwards, who broke the 18-meter barrier in 1995, also illustrate this phenomenon. The triple jump requires extraordinary control of the body, with each phase of the jump - impulsion, stride and final jump - requiring perfect synchronization to maintain momentum and height while covering maximum distance.

These feats, made possible by a unique combination of talent, training and technique, show that even if gravity is an inescapable force, elite athletes sometimes manage to bypass it, if only for a moment, by pushing ever further the limits of what seemed possible.

Fact 82 - Innovative techniques for long jumpers

The techniques used in long jumping have evolved impressively over the decades, enabling athletes to improve their performance dramatically. Perhaps the greatest innovation concerns the timing of the jump. In the past, jumpers focused primarily on speed and momentum, but they soon realized that managing the body in the air was just as crucial to achieving record distances.

Among these techniques, the most revolutionary is the "suspended stride technique", introduced by Jesse Owens in the 1930s. Instead of simply leaping up and hoping for a good landing, Owens made a point of running through the air. This method involved taking strides during flight, giving the impression that he was "running" on an invisible track. Although seemingly simple, this technique maximized body control and extended the distance covered before landing.

Later, jumpers refined this method by developing the "scissor" technique, in which the athlete swings arms and legs synchronously, providing greater stability in flight. This innovation has further perfected flight management, as the body must remain in an aerodynamic position while preparing for an efficient landing. By using this swing, athletes gain precious time in the air, giving them a few extra centimetres.

Another approach that has left its mark on the history of long jumping is that of Carl Lewis, one of the greatest jumpers of all time. Lewis mastered the transition between speed and momentum to perfection, combining incredible running speed with a perfectly synchronized flight phase. He wasn't just fast; he used speed to create a monumental impulse that allowed him to "float" in the air longer than his competitors.

These technical developments show that the long jump is much more than a simple run followed by a jump. Champions of this discipline have constantly sought to improve every aspect of their performance, from impulsion to body management in the air, in order to push back the limits of what is humanly possible.

Fact 83 - Riders who broke records despite their age

In athletics, age is often perceived as an insurmountable obstacle to performance. However, some athletes have defied this preconception, breaking records when many thought their best form was behind them. Their perseverance, rigorous preparation and ironclad mentality have enabled them to reach heights that not even young champions have been able to match.

One of the most striking examples is that of American sprinter Merlene Ottey. Known for her exceptional longevity, she competed in seven Olympic Games, and at the age of 40 was still winning medals at World Championships. Her impeccable technique and ability to remain competitive with younger generations have made her a living legend of athletics. She proves that experience and discipline can surpass the freshness of youth.

In long-distance running, Ethiopian athlete Haile Gebrselassie also left his mark, continuing his career well beyond what many consider the retirement age for elite runners. At over 35, he continued to break world marathon records. His running technique, characterized by a fluid stride and exceptional effort management, enabled him to dominate this discipline even as he passed the age when many athletes hang up their shoes.

Records in athletics are not limited to speed events. Britain's Jo Pavey, a specialist in middle and long-distance running, won international medals in her forties, becoming the oldest person to win a European 10,000-meter title. Her victories are striking proof that intelligent training and experience can compensate for age-related physiological losses.

These champions have shown that tenacity, modern sports science and an extraordinary competitive spirit can keep you at the top, even as you grow older. They inspire not only athletes, but all those who see sport as a means of pushing back their own limits, whatever their age.

Fact 84 - Athletes who have competed in several Olympic Games

Taking part in several Olympic Games is a feat in itself, requiring exceptional consistency in performance, discipline and physical preparation. Some athletes are particularly notable for their longevity, managing to compete in three, four or even five editions of the Olympic Games. Such longevity in a sport as demanding as athletics is rare and testifies to incredible determination.

One of the most impressive examples is Jamaican sprinter Merlene Ottey, who competed in seven Olympic Games between 1980 and 2004. Her endurance at an elite level of performance for more than two decades defied expectations of age and physical ability. Although she never won gold, Ottey went home with nine Olympic medals, making her one of the most decorated athletes in history.

Another outstanding example is that of American shot putter Carl Lewis, who left his mark on the Olympic Games in the 1980s and 1990s. With nine gold medals from four Olympic Games (1984 to 1996), Lewis left an indelible mark on athletics. In particular, he shone in the long jump and the 4x100-meter relay, illustrating not only his versatility but also his longevity in a sport where youth often dominates.

In Africa, Ethiopian long-distance runner Haile Gebrselassie is another example of this Olympic perseverance. Although he shone primarily at the Atlanta Games in 1996 and Sydney in 2000, his Olympic career spans several years with repeated appearances at the Games. His ability to remain competitive despite the changing generations of athletes is impressive, particularly in the long-distance disciplines where physical wear and tear is immense.

These athletes, who have competed in several editions of the Olympic Games, embody the resilience, adaptability and mental strength needed to persist at the highest level of world sport. Not only have they made history with their performances, but they have also inspired generations of athletes to never give up on their dreams, even when time starts to wear on them.

Fact 85 - The role of pacemakers in record-breaking races

Pacemakers, also known as "hares", play a crucial role in record attempts in athletics, particularly in middle and long-distance races. Their mission is to impose a steady pace, enabling runners to stay within the times required to break world records. Although these pacemakers generally don't finish the race, their importance to the success of athletes is immense, and many records would not have been possible without them.

One of the most famous pacemaker contributions took place during the "Breaking2" marathon challenge in 2017. The aim was to run a marathon in under two hours. Although the official record was not recognized by the federation due to the use of these pacemakers, Eliud Kipchoge finished in 2 h 00 min 25 s, thanks to a group of hares taking turns to maintain an ultra-fast and constant pace. This moment demonstrated the direct impact that well-coordinated pacemakers can have on a performance.

The idea of using pacemakers is not new. As early as the 1950s, hares were used in certain races to help athletes set records. One notable example is Roger Bannister, who was the first man to break the four-minute barrier in the mile in 1954. In his historic race, team-mates Chris Brasher and Chris Chataway acted as pacemakers, setting a precise pace on the opening laps.

Pacemakers aren't just fast runners; they need to possess great running intelligence to adjust their pace according to the needs of the main athlete. Their consistency is crucial to maintaining the pace, but they must also know how to withdraw from the race at the right moment, so as not to get in the way of the runner. This role is often assigned to elite runners who, although less famous, possess impeccable technique.

The use of pacemakers remains a subject of debate in the world of athletics, with some believing that it distorts the record-breaking game. However, their undeniable contribution has enabled the history of sport to witness some spectacular moments, and to see barriers once considered insurmountable overcome.

Fact 86 - The oldest athletes to win medals

In the history of the Olympic Games, some athletes have defied time by winning medals at an age when most are already retired. Their sporting longevity and achievements are impressive, testifying to unwavering determination and discipline. One of the most famous examples is Uzbek gymnast Oksana Chusovitina, who took part in eight Olympic Games and won a silver medal at the age of 33, well beyond the average age in her discipline.

In athletics, age was no obstacle for John Akii-Bua, who at the age of 33 won a gold medal in the 400-meter hurdles at the 1972 Olympic Games. Although not the oldest age for an Olympic champion, his performance made history, as he was the first to break 48 seconds over this distance - a rare feat, especially for an athlete of his age.

Marathon runners are also among the oldest medal winners. Long-distance running is often a field where endurance and experience surpass youth. Puerto Rican marathoner Félix Sánchez won a gold medal at the 2012 London Games at the age of 34, an age when many runners have already left the international scene.

An emblematic figure in this category remains Oscar Swahn, a Swedish shooter who is to this day the oldest medallist in the history of the Games. In 1920, at the age of 72, he won a silver medal in a shooting discipline, proving that experience and precision can sometimes be more decisive than physical strength.

These athletes inspire generations, demonstrating that sporting performance is not limited to youth. Their success proves that perseverance, combined with methodical preparation and unwavering passion, can prolong a career well beyond its expected limits, and sometimes lead to Olympic medals, even at an advanced age.

Fact 87 - The secrets of marathon champions' success

The marathon is one of the most demanding disciplines in athletics, and the champions who dominate this race share some well-kept secrets. It all starts with meticulous preparation and training over several years, because the endurance required to run 42.195 km is not acquired quickly. Top athletes like Eliud Kipchoge, for example, spend months fine-tuning their training, including periods at altitude to increase lung capacity and optimize muscle oxygenation.

Diet plays a crucial role in their performance. Marathon champions are careful to maintain a perfect balance between proteins, carbohydrates and fats, while staying rigorously hydrated. One of the best-kept secrets is the management of glycogen reserves, an essential source of energy during the race. Champions like Paula Radcliffe have perfected their nutrition strategy, ensuring rapid recovery after each workout and sufficient energy to sustain their pace throughout the marathon.

The mentality of marathon runners is another decisive factor. For these athletes, mental discipline is just as important as physical preparation. The mind is what keeps them going when their body wants to give up. A champion like Haile Gebrselassie, double Olympic champion, has often mentioned the importance of visualization and the ability to concentrate on each stage of the course, without being overwhelmed by the total distance.

Running economy is also an essential aspect of their success. The best marathon runners perfect their stride to maximize efficiency and reduce energy loss. They also optimize their posture and breathing to minimize fatigue. Eliud Kipchoge, for example, is famous for his fluid stride and consistent pace, which have enabled him to achieve outstanding performances, including becoming the first person to break the two-hour barrier in a marathon.

Finally, support and coaching play a fundamental role. Marathon champions are not alone in their quest for victory. They benefit from the expertise of experienced coaches, specialized doctors and support teams who monitor every detail of their performance. It is this combination of physical, mental, strategic and logistical preparation that enables them to push back the limits of human endurance and write marathon history.

Fact 88 - The longest track and field races ever run

Athletics is not limited to races of a few hundred meters or even marathons. There are endurance competitions that challenge athletes' physical and mental capacities over unimaginable distances. One of the most famous of these is the Spartathlon, a 246 km ultra-marathon race from Athens to Sparta. Inspired by the legendary route of the messenger Phidippides, this race puts runners to the test in terms of heat and difficult terrain.

Another equally impressive race is the Badwater Ultramarathon. Run in California's Death Valley over a distance of 217 km, it is renowned for its extreme weather conditions. Temperatures can reach 50°C, and the course includes significant elevation changes, ranging from 85 meters below sea level to over 2,500 meters above sea level. Participants not only have to contend with muscular fatigue, but also rapid dehydration and the risk of heatstroke.

The 24-hour ultramarathon, although shorter in distance, poses a different kind of challenge. In these races, athletes must run as much as possible in a full day, often on repetitive circuits of just a few kilometers. The record for distance covered in 24 hours is over 300 km, achieved by runners such as Yiannis Kouros, renowned for his exceptional performances over very long distances.

Some races go even further, like the Self-Transcendence 3100 Mile Race, which is the longest certified race in the world, with 4,988 km to cover. This race takes place in New York and requires participants to cover almost 100 km a day for several weeks, often on monotonous courses of a few hundred meters around a single city block. Few athletes dare attempt this extreme event, which requires exceptional physical preparation and unshakeable mental strength.

These races, which push the limits of human endurance, demonstrate that athletics goes far beyond explosive sprints and fast records. They illustrate the ability of runners to defy the body's physical boundaries and transcend fatigue, exhaustion and sometimes even pain to achieve almost superhuman feats.

Fact 89 - World records in discus throwing

Discus throwing is one of the oldest disciplines in athletics, dating back to ancient Greece, but its modern records testify to the incredible power and technique of today's athletes. The men's world record, held by Jürgen Schult, was set in 1986 with a throw of 74.08 meters. This record, unmatched for decades, remains a milestone in the history of the sport, demonstrating exceptional mastery of the spinning motion and explosive force required to propel the discus over such a distance.

To achieve such performances, discus throwers combine strength, speed and precision. The secret lies in the ability to generate maximum power at the moment of pivot and release the discus with perfect trajectory. International competitions show just how crucial this balance between technique and strength is. Weather conditions also play an important role: a favorable wind can add precious centimeters to the throw, while contrary gusts can ruin a promising attempt.

The women's world record is held by Gabriele Reinsch, with an impressive throw of 76.80 metres in 1988. This record, too, has remained unbroken ever since, showing just how difficult these performances are to achieve. Current training techniques, though sophisticated, struggle to surpass these incredible results. Today's athletes are improving by integrating biomechanical techniques and maximizing their explosiveness with every throw, but the marks set in the 80s remain a benchmark.

Discus throwing technique has evolved over time, from a simple throw to a complex rotation that allows athletes to optimize the force generated by their body. Today's champions spend hours perfecting every stage of their movement: from the initial swing to the rotation, right up to the decisive moment when the discus leaves the hand. Every fraction of a second is crucial to achieving those legendary distances.

Discus throwing, while a spectacle of brute strength, is above all a demonstration of balance and technical mastery. The men's and women's world records are a tribute to years of hard training and perfected technique, and they continue to inspire future generations to push the boundaries of what is possible in this fascinating discipline.

Fact 90 - The fastest races on soggy tracks

Adverse weather conditions, such as a rain-soaked track, can radically affect athletes' performances. Yet some sprinters have managed to shine even in the pouring rain. One of the most memorable races in these conditions took place at the 1993 World Athletics Championships in Stuttgart. On that day, Michael Johnson, one of the best sprinters of all time, dominated the 400-meter race in the pouring rain, posting an impressive time despite the slippery track.

The key to these performances often lies in technique and concentration. Running on a wet track requires extra vigilance with every step, as grip is reduced, and a false move can lead to a loss of speed or even a fall. Athletes learn to adapt their stride, avoiding slips and maintaining optimum stability, while keeping their pace. Runners like Usain Bolt and Shelly-Ann Fraser-Pryce have also demonstrated their ability to maintain blistering speeds even in rainy conditions at international competitions.

Equipment quality also plays a crucial role. Spiked shoes, specifically designed to offer better grip on wet tracks, enable athletes to maintain powerful propulsion without losing control. At the 2016 Rio Olympics, the men's 4x100-meter relay was run in relentless rain, but that didn't stop the Jamaicans from taking gold, with impressive speed that seemed to defy the elements.

Despite these challenges, some races in the rain have even led to astonishing records. Athletes who excel in such conditions demonstrate exceptional adaptability, uncommon mental strength and rigorous training. Their exploits will always be remembered, for they embody the very essence of athletics: resilience, speed and body control in the face of all adversity.

These performances are a reminder that, despite adverse circumstances, athletics is a sport where every race counts and where weather conditions do not hinder the quest for victory.

Fact 91 - The world's best sprinters in 2020

The year 2020, although marked by the pandemic, has not prevented some of the world's greatest sprinters from continuing to impress on the track. Among them, American Noah Lyles stood out with his exceptional performances. A 200-meter specialist, he continued to dominate his discipline with explosive speed and refined technique, culminating in a time of 19.76 seconds in 2020. His fluid style and incredible mastery of the final meters put him at the pinnacle of world sprinting.

In the 100 m, Christian Coleman, also American, marked the year with some dazzling performances. Despite facing a suspension for failing to comply with his whereabouts obligations, Coleman still held the world's best 100 m performance with a time of 9.76 seconds. His ability to generate maximum speed from the very first meters made him a favorite for international podiums.

On the women's side, Jamaica's Shelly-Ann Fraser-Pryce proved she's still one of the best. At the age of 33, she continued to run at an incredible level, claiming 100 m victories with times under 11 seconds, while inspiring a new generation of athletes. Her steely mentality and unrivalled technique made her a sprint legend, still as competitive as ever despite the years.

South African sprinter Akani Simbine also made his mark in 2020 with remarkable performances, notably in Europe, clocking times close to 9.91 seconds over 100m. Considered one of Africa's best sprinters, he maintained a high standard despite the difficult conditions, consolidating his place among the world's elite.

Despite the uncertainties of 2020, these sprinters have continued to push the boundaries of world sprinting. Their performances, whether in terms of times achieved or technical mastery, embody the pinnacle of modern athletics, proving that even in troubled times, talent and hard work always triumph.

Fact 92 - Decathlon performances through the decades

The decathlon is often regarded as the premier discipline in athletics, testing athletes' versatility, strength, speed and endurance. Since the event's debut at the 1912 Olympic Games, decathletes have consistently pushed the limits of human performance. Jim Thorpe, considered the first great decathlon champion, marked the 1910s with exceptional versatility, winning the discipline's first Olympic title in Stockholm.

The following decades saw the emergence of iconic figures such as Bob Mathias, who dominated the discipline in the 1940s and 1950s, winning two Olympic gold medals. Impressively, he won his first title at just 17, becoming the youngest male Olympic champion in history. The 1960s and 1970s saw the rise of Bruce Jenner (now Caitlyn Jenner), who won gold in Montreal in 1976, with an overall performance that is remembered as a turning point in decathlon history.

With the arrival of Daley Thompson in the 1980s, the standard of decathlon was raised once again. The British athlete dominated the world stage, winning back-to-back Olympic titles in 1980 and 1984. His ability to excel in all ten disciplines, combined with exceptional mental toughness, made him a role model for future generations. Thompson also popularized the idea that the decathlon was not just about physics, but also about strategy and effort management.

Decathlon world records have continued to be improved over the decades, culminating with American Ashton Eaton in the 2010s. Eaton redefined the standards by breaking the world record twice, in 2012 and 2015, reaching a total of 9045 points, a feat rarely equalled in the sport's history. His unique combination of 100-meter speed, explosiveness in the long jump and consistency in other events has made him one of the greatest decathletes of all time.

Over the decades, the performances of decathletes have reflected the evolution of athletics in terms of technique, training and mental preparation. What hasn't changed is the spirit of surpassing oneself that drives these athletes to give their best in ten disciplines as varied as sprinting, throwing and jumping.

Fact 93 - The longest long jump of all time

The long jump is one of the most impressive disciplines in athletics, where precision and power are essential to achieve dizzying distances. Mike Powell's performance at the 1991 World Athletics Championships in Tokyo remains one of the sport's most memorable. Powell jumped 8.95 meters, beating Bob Beamon's legendary record, which had stood since the 1968 Olympic Games. The jump is still recognized as the longest ever recorded in competition.

This record is all the more remarkable in that it was achieved under extremely competitive conditions. That day, Carl Lewis, his direct rival, was stringing together spectacular jumps and seemed unbeatable. Powell, aware of the difficulty of the task, found the mental and physical strength to execute a perfect jump at the crucial moment. With an impeccable run-up, explosive release and ideal flight posture, he not only broke the record, but also made track and field history.

Powell's performance was impressive not only for the distance he reached, but also for his technical mastery of the gesture. The long jump requires maximum speed at the moment of impulse, while controlling every millimeter of the foot to avoid a false start. Powell executed this complex combination with unrivalled precision, his jump becoming a technical benchmark for subsequent generations.

Even with advances in training and technology, this 1991 record remains inviolate to this day. Many elite athletes have attempted to approach this mythical mark, but no one has yet managed to surpass Powell's 8.95 meters. The record symbolizes the human limit in this discipline, showing that certain performances remain engraved in time.

Mike Powell's jump continues to inspire athletes the world over. Every new generation of long jumpers dreams of reproducing this extraordinary feat. But beyond the distance, it's the combination of talent, perseverance and perfect timing that makes this jump a true legend of world athletics.

Fact 94 - Running techniques that improve speed

The quest for speed in athletics is not just about muscular strength or endurance. The best sprinters master specific running techniques that enable them to gain precious hundredths of a second. Among these techniques, body posture is paramount. A slightly forward-leaning body, with perfect alignment of head, torso and hips, reduces air resistance and promotes more efficient acceleration.

Foot placement also plays a crucial role. To maximize propulsion, it's essential to place the foot under the body's center of gravity, rather than forward. This avoids braking with every stride and fully exploits the kinetic energy accumulated during the run-up. Elite runners train to increase cadence while reducing ground contact time, a decisive factor in optimizing speed.

Breathing is often underestimated, but it's just as important. Controlled breathing, which allows maximum oxygenation of the muscles, helps maintain an explosive effort throughout a sprint. Sprinters learn to synchronize their breathing with their strides, enabling them to remain powerful even in the final meters of a race.

Another key element is arm coordination. Contrary to what you might think, arm movement plays an essential role in propulsion and balance. Arms that swing quickly and at the right angle generate a counter-force that allows the legs to move more efficiently. Trainers make a point of correcting arm technique to avoid any loss of speed.

Mental training complements this physical approach. The ability to visualize an explosive start, fluid acceleration and powerful finish can make all the difference in a competition. Elite athletes train not only to rehearse the right moves, but also to condition their minds to stay focused and perform under pressure. This combination of technique, strategy and mental preparation explains why some racers manage to constantly push back the limits of human speed.

Fact 95 - The longest winning streaks in athletics

In the history of athletics, certain series of victories have become legendary, illustrating the absolute domination of certain athletes over a discipline. One of the most impressive is that of Edwin Moses, undisputed master of the 400-meter hurdles. Between 1977 and 1987, Moses won 122 consecutive races, setting an almost unrivalled record for consistency and mastery in his discipline. This series illustrates not only his talent, but also his incredible mental and physical preparation.

Another outstanding example is that of Soviet-Russian pole vaulter Yelena Isinbayeva, whose string of victories and records in the pole vault has left a lasting impression. Between 2004 and 2009, she not only dominated her rivals, but also raised the standard of the discipline by breaking numerous world records, consolidating her status as a living legend of the pole vault.

Kenyan long-distance runner Eliud Kipchoge also deserves a mention. Considered the greatest marathoner of all time, Kipchoge has won 10 marathons in a row, from 2014 to 2019. His absolute domination of this event, often considered the most demanding in athletics, shows just how crucial physical preparation, race strategy and resilience are in such long disciplines.

Florence Griffith-Joyner, known as Flo-Jo, made her mark at the 1988 Seoul Olympic Games with a series of spectacular victories in the 100 and 200 meters, shattering the world records of the time. Her performances remain unrivalled to this day, and her name is associated with the perfection of women's sprinting.

These winning streaks are built not just on talent, but also on hard work, rigorous discipline and an ability to maintain incredible consistency. Across decades and continents, these champions have redefined the standards of athletics, leaving an indelible mark on the history of the sport.

Fact 96 - Athletes' exploits at the Summer Olympics

The Summer Olympics have always been a stage for some of the most impressive feats in the history of athletics. One of the most memorable moments was Jesse Owens' performance at the 1936 Berlin Games. By winning four gold medals in the sprint and long jump, he defied not only his opponents, but also the racial ideologies of the time, becoming a living legend of athletics.

In 1968, at the Olympic Games in Mexico City, Bob Beamon produced a prodigious long jump that pushed back the boundaries of the discipline. With a leap of 8.90 meters, he shattered the previous world record by almost 55 centimeters. This jump is still regarded today as one of the greatest feats ever achieved in athletics, so much so that the expression "doing a Beamon" has entered the vocabulary to describe a record that is difficult to match.

Women's achievements were not to be outdone. At the 1984 Los Angeles Games, Carl Lewis, often compared to Owens, matched the latter's feat by winning four gold medals in the same disciplines. This performance catapulted him to world stardom and consolidated his status as the best sprinter and long jumper of his generation. As for Florence Griffith-Joyner, she stunned the world with her crushing victories and unsurpassed records in the 100 and 200 meters.

More recently, Ugandan Stephen Kiprotich caused a sensation in London 2012 by winning gold in the marathon. His feat was all the more remarkable given that he was not the favorite, but shone in one of the most physically demanding events of the Olympic Games. This event reminded us all that sport remains unpredictable and that every race has its surprises in store.

Every Summer Olympic Games is an opportunity for athletes to surpass their limits and make history. These legendary feats continue to inspire generations of athletes to pursue excellence.

Fact 97 - The greatest track and field performances of the decade

Over the last decade, track and field has seen performances that have redefined the boundaries of the sport, making history. Among these unforgettable moments, Usain Bolt solidified his place as the greatest sprinter of all time. With his world records still intact in the 100 and 200 metres, notably his 9.58 seconds in 2009, he has inspired generations of athletes to strive for excellence in a fiercely competitive discipline.

In 2019, Eliud Kipchoge broke a barrier that many thought was insurmountable. At the INEOS 1:59 event in Vienna, he became the first man to run a marathon in under two hours. Although this performance is not recognized as an official record due to the optimized conditions, it remains one of the most impressive in the history of athletics, proving that human endurance can reach unsuspected heights.

On the women's side, Almaz Ayana made her mark on the 2016 Rio Olympics by breaking the world record in the 10,000 meters with a time of 29:17.45. She shattered a 23-year-old record, overtaking her competitors by a staggering margin. This performance resonated around the world, highlighting the exceptional talent of this Ethiopian athlete and demonstrating that historic records can still be broken.

Pole vaulting also saw a major upheaval. Armand "Mondo" Duplantis, the young Swedish prodigy, has broken the world record several times this decade, culminating in a jump of 6.18 meters in 2020. His technical mastery and youthfulness suggest that he could go even further, but he is already establishing himself as the new master of the discipline.

These landmark performances not only shook up the statistics, but also inspired new generations of athletes to aim ever higher and further. The last decade has proved that athletics is a constantly evolving sport, where human limits are constantly being pushed back.

Fact 98 - Olympic champions who made sprinting history

Ever since the first modern Olympic Games, sprinting has been track and field's premier discipline, producing champions who have left their mark on the history of the sport. Jesse Owens, at the Berlin Games in 1936, embodies the moment when athletics transcended sport. He won four gold medals in a tense political climate, demonstrating the power of sprinting to convey messages far beyond the track.

More recently, Usain Bolt has become a living legend of the sprint. Three-time Olympic champion in the 100 and 200 metres (2008, 2012, 2016), the Jamaican holds the world records in both distances. His relaxed style and incredible top speed have not only impressed the world, but also changed the perception of what human beings can achieve in athletics. Bolt has left an indelible mark on the history of the Olympic Games.

Carl Lewis, another key figure in sprinting, won nine Olympic gold medals between 1984 and 1996, consolidating his status as one of the greatest athletes of all time. His duel with Ben Johnson in Seoul in 1988, though tarnished by the doping scandal, remains one of the most memorable moments in Olympic history. Lewis's longevity and ability to excel in multiple disciplines make him a legend in his own right.

On the women's side, Florence Griffith-Joyner, nicknamed "Flo-Jo", shone at the 1988 Seoul Games. Her world records in the 100 and 200 metres, set that year, are still untouched. Her flamboyant style, with colorful outfits and extravagant nails, only reinforced her image as an iconic Olympic champion, combining speed and personality.

These athletes redefined the boundaries of Olympic sprinting, each in their own way. They not only broke records, but also captured the public's imagination, inspiring generations of young sprinters to dream of conquering Olympic gold. Their exploits continue to resonate in the history of sport, bearing witness to timeless sporting excellence.

Fact 99 - The fastest relay races of 2010

The relay races of the 2010s were marked by intensity and spectacular performances, particularly in the 4x100 metres and 4x400 metres. One of the most dominant teams of the decade was the Jamaican team, led by Usain Bolt. At the 2012 London Olympics, the Jamaican relay set a memorable world record of 36.84 seconds in the 4x100m, a feat that has yet to be surpassed. The perfect coordination of the baton passes and the incredible speed of the sprinters made this race a historic moment.

The USA also shone during this period, particularly in the 4x400m relay. At the 2011 World Championships in Daegu, the American team showed their supremacy by winning gold with a time of 2:59.31. Their ability to maintain exceptional speed throughout the four laps solidified their place as one of the best relay runners of the decade. 4x400m races demand impeccable endurance and strategy, and the Americans proved that they have mastered these elements to perfection.

At the same time, the women delivered equally impressive performances. In 2012, the US women's 4x100m team broke a 27-year-old world record at the London Games, running 40.82 seconds. The coordination between Carmelita Jeter, Allyson Felix, Tianna Madison and Bianca Knight achieved a feat few thought possible. The relay remains one of the fastest and most iconic in history.

The British team has also made its mark in this decade. At the 2017 World Championships, Great Britain's men's 4x100m relay stunned by winning the gold medal in 37.47 seconds. This unexpected triumph put an end to Jamaica's hegemony, and the success was largely attributed to flawless execution of the baton passes, proving that individual talent must be supported by impeccable technique.

The relay races of the 2010s not only brought new records, they also showed the importance of team cohesion, sheer speed and strategy. These relays, with their moments of tension and triumph, marked an era when human speed seemed to be constantly pushing its own limits.

Fact 100 - Olympic champions with the most world records

Olympic champions who hold multiple world records embody a form of absolute domination in athletics. Usain Bolt, the "King of Sprint", is one of the greatest examples. With his outstanding performances in the 100m and 200m, he not only won three consecutive gold medals at the Olympic Games, but also set legendary world records, including his 9.58 seconds in the 100m and 19.19 seconds in the 200m at the 2009 World Championships.

Carl Lewis, another sprint and long jump legend, has left a lasting imprint on Olympic and world records. With nine Olympic gold medals to his credit, he also broke numerous world records in these disciplines. His longevity and versatility enabled him to remain competitive at the highest level for almost a decade, a rare feat in a field where speed and precision reign supreme.

In swimming, we can't talk about world records without mentioning the American Michael Phelps, holder of the most Olympic swimming records. Although swimming is different from athletics, his influence and incredible number of records have inspired many athletes, particularly in track and field, to push their own limits. The parallels between his and Bolt's domination of their respective disciplines are striking.

On the women's side, sprinter Florence Griffith-Joyner, nicknamed "Flo Jo", shook the stopwatches in 1988 with her world records in the 100m (10.49 seconds) and 200m (21.34 seconds), times that have never been beaten. Her unique technique and explosiveness redefined what female athletes could achieve in athletics, setting the bar incredibly high for future generations.

These athletes didn't just compete or win medals; they transformed their sport. Each record broken represents years of hard training, technical innovation and mental discipline. Their feats have inspired millions to believe that even the most extreme limits can be overcome.

Conclusion

After exploring these 100 Amazing Facts about athletics, you now have an overview of the key moments that have shaped this exciting sport. From Dick Fosbury's revolutionary leap to Eliud Kipchoge's legendary endurance, you've discovered human performances that defy physical and mental limits.

Athletics never stops renewing itself. Each generation of athletes brings its own innovations and new records, but it's the stories behind these feats that make the sport so captivating. You've read these stories and understood the importance of commitment, discipline and hard work.

Through these pages, you've also discovered that athletics is more than just a competition. It's a human adventure where technology, history and culture come together to create a universal spectacle. Records aren't just numbers, they tell stories of overcoming adversity.

Closing this book may give you a new perspective on athletics. Perhaps you'll be inspired to strap on a pair of sneakers and try to push yourself to the limit. Whatever the case, these Facts will remain a source of wonder for sports enthusiasts, and a constant reminder of the incredible potential of the human body.

Athletics, in all its splendor, continues to show us that the impossible is within reach. Each generation writes a new chapter, and who knows, maybe you'll be part of the next great story to be told.

Marc Dresqui

Quiz

1) What was the distance of the first official hurdling competition in England in 1864?

- a)   100 meters
- b)   150 yards
- c)   120 yards
- d)   110 meters

2) How high did Dick Fosbury jump to win the gold medal in the high jump at the 1968 Olympic Games?

- a)   2.30 metres
- b)   2.24 metres
- c)   2.20 metres
- d)   2.18 metres

3) Which model of running shoe helped Eliud Kipchoge set the marathon world record in 2018?

- a)   Adidas Ultraboost
- b)   Nike Vaporfly
- c)   New Balance Fresh Foam
- d)   Puma Speed

4) Why is the current marathon distance set at 42.195 kilometers?

- a)   To commemorate the legend of Philippides
- b)   Because it was the distance of the first Olympic race in 1896
- c)   Due to a modification of the course during the 1908 London Olympic Games
- d)   To harmonize world marathon distances

5) Which long jumper broke Bob Beamon's famous 1968 record?

- a)   Carl Lewis
- b)   Mike Powell
- c)   Jesse Owens
- d)   Usain Bolt

6) What is the typical reaction time range of the best sprinters at the start?

- a)   0.10 to 0.12 seconds
- b)   0.15 to 0.18 seconds
- c)   0.20 to 0.25 seconds
- d)   0.30 to 0.35 seconds

7) Which surface was used for the first time at the 1968 Olympic Games in Mexico City, revolutionizing runners' performances?

a) Clay
b) Sand
c) Tartan
d) Ash

8) Which long-jump technique used in the 90s consisted of leg movements in the air to extend flight time?

a) Group jump
b) Scissors jump
c) Hitch-kick
d) Ventral impulse

9) At which event did Colin Jackson break the 110-meter hurdles world record in the rain?

a) Beijing 2008 Olympic Games
b) 1993 Stuttgart World Championships
c) Tokyo 1964 Olympic Games
d) Olympic Games Mexico 1968

10) Which coach played a decisive role in Usain Bolt's career, helping him become the greatest sprinter of all time?

a) Percy Cerutty
b) Bob Kersee
c) Glen Mills
d) Alberto Salazar

11) Which athlete is the youngest to have taken part in the Olympic Games, aged just 10?

a) Merlene Ottey
b) Sydney McLaughlin
c) Cheng Yung-chien
d) Dimitrios Loundras

12) Which decathlete broke the world record in 2015 with a total of 9045 points?

a) Kevin Mayer
b) Roman Šebrle
c) Ashton Eaton
d) Daley Thompson

13) Which athlete holds the world record for the greatest distance covered in 24 hours, with 303.506 km?

a) Scott Jurek

b) Kilian Jornet
c) Yiannis Kouros
d) Dean Karnazes

14) At which famous Olympic race in 1960 was the photo finish used to declare Armin Hary the winner of the 100-metre race?

a) The London Olympics
b) The Tokyo Olympic Games
c) The Olympic Games in Rome
d) The Munich Olympic Games

15) Which runner is known for his meditative calm and mastery of endurance in long-distance races?

a) Haile Gebrselassie
b) Kilian Jornet
c) Eliud Kipchoge
d) Mo Farah

16) Which athlete still holds the men's javelin-throwing world record today, with a throw of 98.48 metres?

a) Barbora Špotáková
b) Jan Železný
c) Andreas Thorkildsen
d) Julius Yego

17) Which athlete was helped by pacemakers in the "Breaking2" challenge to run a marathon in under two hours?

a) Roger Bannister
b) Eliud Kipchoge
c) Mo Farah
d) Kenenisa Bekele

18) Which athlete holds the men's discus world record with a throw of 74.08 metres?

a) Virgilijus Alekna
b) Gerd Kanter
c) Jürgen Schult
d) Robert Harting

19) Which athlete won 122 consecutive races in the 400-meter hurdles between 1977 and 1987?

a) Yelena Isinbayeva
b) Edwin Moses
c) Eliud Kipchoge
d) Florence Griffith-Joyner

20) Which Olympic champion holds the 100m and 200m world records with legendary performances of 9.58 seconds and 19.19 seconds?

    a)   Carl Lewis
    b)   Michael Phelps
    c)   Florence Griffith-Joyner
    d)   Usain Bolt

Answers

1) What was the distance of the first official hurdling competition in England in 1864?

Correct answer: c) 120 yards

2) How high did Dick Fosbury jump to win the gold medal in the high jump at the 1968 Olympic Games?

Correct answer: b) 2.24 metres

3) Which model of running shoe helped Eliud Kipchoge set the marathon world record in 2018?

Correct answer: b) Nike Vaporfly

4) Why is the current marathon distance set at 42.195 kilometers?

Correct answer: c) Because of a change to the course at the 1908 London Olympics.

5) Which long jumper broke Bob Beamon's famous 1968 record?

Correct answer: b) Mike Powell

6) What is the typical reaction time range of the best sprinters at the start?

Correct answer: b) 0.15 to 0.18 seconds

7) Which surface was used for the first time at the 1968 Olympic Games in Mexico City, revolutionizing runners' performances?

Correct answer: c) Tartan

8) Which long jump technique used in the 90's consisted of leg movements in the air to extend flight time?

Correct answer: c) Hitch-kick

9) At which event did Colin Jackson break the 110-meter hurdles world record in the rain?

Correct answer: b) 1993 Stuttgart World Championships

10) Which coach played a decisive role in Usain Bolt's career, helping him become the greatest sprinter of all time?

Correct answer: c) Glen Mills

11) Which athlete is the youngest to have taken part in the Olympic Games, aged just 10?

Correct answer: d) Dimitrios Loundras

12) Which decathlete broke the world record in 2015 with a total of 9045 points?

Correct answer: c) Ashton Eaton

13) Which athlete holds the world record for the greatest distance covered in 24 hours, with 303.506 km?

Correct answer: c) Yiannis Kouros

14) At which famous Olympic race in 1960 was the photo finish used to declare Armin Hary the winner of the 100-metre race?

Correct answer: c) The Olympic Games in Rome

15) Which runner is known for his meditative calm and mastery of endurance in long-distance races?

Correct answer: c) Eliud Kipchoge

16) Which athlete still holds the men's javelin-throwing world record today, with a throw of 98.48 metres?

Correct answer: b) Jan Železný

17) Which athlete was helped by pacemakers in the "Breaking2" challenge to run a marathon in under two hours?

Correct answer: b) Eliud Kipchoge

18) Which athlete holds the men's discus world record with a throw of 74.08 metres?

Correct answer: c) Jürgen Schult

19) Which athlete won 122 consecutive races in the 400-meter hurdles between 1977 and 1987?

Correct answer: b) Edwin Moses

20) Which Olympic champion holds the 100m and 200m world records with legendary performances of 9.58 seconds and 19.19 seconds?

Correct answer: d) Usain Bolt

Printed in Great Britain
by Amazon

55789141R00069